About the

Róman Joost is a professional Python software developer and a free software enthusiast, currently living in Australia. Since 2003, he has been contributing to the GNU Image Manipulation Program (GIMP) by writing documentation and contributing to the source code. He uses testing frameworks and test-driven methodologies extensively, when writing new components for the Z Object Publishing Environment (Zope) in Python.

Andrew Nicholson is a software engineer with over 12 years of professional commercial experience in a broad range of technologies. He is passionate about free and open source software (FOSS) and has actively participated in contributing code, ideas, and passion in the open source community since 1999.

Nicholson's biography can be read at http://infiniterecursion.com.au/people/.

Herjend Teny is an electrical engineering graduate from Melbourne who has come to love programming in Python after years of programming in mainline programming languages, such as C, Java, and Pascal.

He is currently involved in designing web application using Django for an Article Repository project on http://www.havingfunwithlinux.com/. The project would allow users to post their article for public view and bookmark it onto their favorite blog.

Table of Contents

Preface

Like any programmer, you need to be able to produce reliable code that conforms to a specification, which means that you need to test your code. In this book, you'll learn how to use techniques and Python tools that reduce the effort involved in testing, and at the same time make it more useful—and even fun.

You'll learn about several of Python's automated testing tools, and you'll learn about the philosophies and methodologies that they were designed to support, like unit testing and test-driven development. When you're done, you'll be able to produce thoroughly tested code faster and more easily than ever before, and you'll be able to do it in a way that doesn't distract you from your "real" programming.

What this book covers

Chapter 1: *Testing for Fun and Profit* introduces Python test-driven development and various testing methods.

Chapter 2: *Doctest: The Easiest Testing Tool* covers the doctest tool and teaches you how to use it.

Chapter 3: *Unit Testing with Doctest* introduces the ideas of unit testing and test-driven development, and applies doctest to create unit tests.

Chapter 4: *Breaking Tight Coupling by using Mock Objects* covers mock objects and the Python Mocker tool.

Chapter 5: *When Doctest isn't Enough: Unittest to the Rescue* introduces the unittest framework and discusses when it is preferred over doctest.

Chapter 6: *Running Your Tests: Follow Your Nose* introduces the Nose test runner, and discusses project organization.

Chapter 7: *Developing a Test-Driven Project* walks through a complete test-driven development process.

Chapter 8: *Testing Web Application Frontends using Twill* applies the knowledge gained from previous chapters to web applications, and introduces the Twill tool.

Chapter 9: *Integration Testing and System Testing* teaches how to build from unit tests to tests of a complete software system.

Chapter 10: *Other Testing Tools and Techniques* introduces code coverage and continuous integration, and teaches how to tie automated testing into version control systems.

Appendix: *Answers to Pop Quizes* contains the answers to all pop quizes, chapter-wise.

What you need for this book

To use this book, you will need a working Python interpreter, preferably one of the 2.6 version series. You'll also need a source code editor, and occasional access to the internet. You will need to be comfortable enough using your operating system's textual interface—your DOS prompt or command shell—to do basic directory management and to run programs.

Who this book is for

If you are a Python developer and want to write tests for your applications, this book will get you started and show you the easiest way to learn testing.

You need to have sound Python programming knowledge to follow along. An awareness of software testing would be good, but no formal knowledge of testing is expected nor do you need to have any knowledge of the libraries discussed in the book.

Conventions

In this book, you will find several headings appearing frequently.

To give clear instructions of how to complete a procedure or task, we use:

Time for action – heading

1. Action 1
2. Action 2
3. Action 3

Instructions often need some extra explanation so that they make sense, so they are followed with:

What just happened?

This heading explains the working of tasks or instructions that you have just completed.

You will also find some other learning aids in the book, including:

Pop quiz – heading

These are short multiple choice questions intended to help you test your own understanding.

Have a go hero – heading

These set practical challenges and give you ideas for experimenting with what you have learned.

You will also find a number of styles of text that distinguish between different kinds of information. Here are some examples of these styles, and an explanation of their meaning.

Code words in text are shown as follows: "We can include other contexts through the use of the include directive."

A block of code is set as follows:

```
...         if node.right is not None:
...             assert isinstance(node.right, AVL)
...             assert node.right.key > node.key
...             right_height = node.right.height + 1
```

When we wish to draw your attention to a particular part of a code block, the relevant lines or items are set in bold:

```
...         if node.right is not None:
...             assert isinstance(node.right, AVL)
...             assert node.right.key > node.key
...             right_height = node.right.height + 1
```

Any command-line input or output is written as follows:

```
# cp /usr/src/asterisk-addons/configs/cdr_mysql.conf.sample
   /etc/asterisk/cdr_mysql.conf
```

New terms and **important words** are shown in bold. Words that you see on the screen, in menus or dialog boxes for example, appear in the text like this: "clicking the Next button moves you to the next screen".

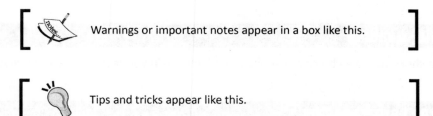

Warnings or important notes appear in a box like this.

Tips and tricks appear like this.

Reader feedback

Feedback from our readers is always welcome. Let us know what you think about this book—what you liked or may have disliked. Reader feedback is important for us to develop titles that you really get the most out of.

To send us general feedback, simply send an email to feedback@packtpub.com, and mention the book title via the subject of your message.

If there is a book that you need and would like to see us publish, please send us a note in the **SUGGEST A TITLE** form on www.packtpub.com or email suggest@packtpub.com.

If there is a topic that you have expertise in and you are interested in either writing or contributing to a book on, see our author guide on www.packtpub.com/authors.

Customer support

Now that you are the proud owner of a Packt book, we have a number of things to help you to get the most from your purchase.

Downloading the example code for the book

Visit http://www.packtpub.com/files/code/8846_Code.zip to directly download the example code.

The downloadable files contain instructions on how to use them.

Errata

Although we have taken every care to ensure the accuracy of our content, mistakes do happen. If you find a mistake in one of our books—maybe a mistake in the text or the code—we would be grateful if you would report this to us. By doing so, you can save other readers from frustration, and help us to improve subsequent versions of this book. If you find any errata, please report them by visiting http://www.packtpub.com/support, selecting your book, clicking on the **let us know** link, and entering the details of your errata. Once your errata are verified, your submission will be accepted and the errata added to any list of existing errata. Any existing errata can be viewed by selecting your title from `http://www.packtpub.com/support`.

Piracy

Piracy of copyright material on the Internet is an ongoing problem across all media. At Packt, we take the protection of our copyright and licenses very seriously. If you come across any illegal copies of our works, in any form, on the Internet, please provide us with the location address or web site name immediately so that we can pursue a remedy.

Please contact us at `copyright@packtpub.com` with a link to the suspected pirated material.

We appreciate your help in protecting our authors, and our ability to bring you valuable content.

Questions

You can contact us at `questions@packtpub.com` if you are having a problem with any aspect of the book, and we will do our best to address it.

1

Testing for Fun and Profit

You're a programmer: a coder, a developer, or maybe a hacker! As such, it's almost impossible that you haven't had to sit down with a program that you were sure was ready for use—or worse yet, a program you knew was not ready—and put together a bunch of tests to prove it. It often feels like an exercise in futility, or at best a waste of time. We'll learn how to avoid that situation, and make testing an easy and enjoyable process.

This book is going to show you a new way to test, a way that puts much of the burden of testing right where it should be: on the computer. Even better, your tests will help you to find problems early and tell you just where they are, so that you can fix them easily. You'll love the easy, helpful methods of automated testing and test-driven development that you will learn about in this book.

The Python language has some of the best tools available, when it comes to testing. As a result, we'll learn how to make testing something that is easy, quick, and fun by taking advantage of those tools.

In this book, we'll:

◆ Study popular testing tools such as doctest, unittest, and Nose

◆ Learn about testing philosophies like unit testing and test-driven development

◆ Examine the use of mock objects and other useful testing secrets

◆ Learn how to integrate testing with the other tools that we use, and with our workflow

◆ Introduce some secondary tools that make it easier to use the major testing tools

How can testing help?

This chapter started with a lot of grandiose claims, such as: You'll enjoy testing. You'll rely on it to help you kill bugs early and easily. Testing will stop being a burden for you, and become something that you want to do. You may be wondering how this is possible?

Think back to the last annoying bug that you had to deal with. It could have been anything; a database schema mismatch, or a bad data structure.

Remember what caused the bug? The one line of code with a subtle logic error? The function that didn't do what the documents said it would do? Whatever it was, keep it in mind.

Imagine a small chunk of code that could have caught the bug, if it had been run at the right time, and informed you about it.

Now imagine that all of your code was accompanied by those little chunks of test code, and that they are quick and easy to execute.

How long would your bug have survived? Not very long at all.

That gives you a basic understanding of what we'll be talking about in this book. There are many tools and refinements that can make the process quicker and easier. The basic idea is to tell the computer what you expect, using simple and easily-written chunks of code, and then have the computer double-check your expectations throughout the coding process. As expectations are easy to describe, you can write them down first, allowing the computer to shoulder much of the burden of debugging your code. As a result, you can move on to interesting things while the computer keeps a track of everything else.

When you're done, you'll have a code base that is highly tested and that you can be confident in. You will have caught your bugs early and fixed them quickly. The best part is that your testing was done by the computer based on what you told it you wanted the program to do. After all, why should you do it, when the computer can do it for you?

I have programmed simple automated tests to catch everything from minor typos, to instances of database access code being left dangerously out of date after a schema change, and pretty much any other bug you can imagine. The tests caught the errors quickly, and pinpointed their locations. A great deal of effort and bother was avoided because they were there.

Imagine the time that you'll save or spend on writing new features, instead of chasing old bugs. Better code, written more quickly, has a good cost/benefit ratio. Testing the right way really is both more fun and more profitable.

Types of testing

Testing is commonly divided into several categories, based on how complex the component being tested is. Most of our time will be focused on the lowest level—unit testing—because tests in the other categories operate on pretty much the same principles.

Unit testing

Unit testing is testing of the smallest possible pieces of a program. Often, this means individual functions or methods. The keyword here is individual; something is a *unit* if it there's no meaningful way to divide it up further.

Unit tests are used to test a single unit in isolation, verifying that it works as expected, without considering what the rest of the program would do. This protects each unit from inheriting bugs from mistakes made elsewhere, and makes it easy to narrow down on the actual problem.

By itself, unit testing isn't enough to confirm that a complete program works correctly, but it's the foundation upon which everything else is based. You can't build a house without solid materials, and you can't build a program without units that work as expected!

Integration testing

In integration testing, the boundaries of isolation are pushed further back, so that the tests encompass interactions between related units. Each test should still be run in isolation, to avoid inheriting problems from outside, but now the test checks whether the tested units behave correctly as a group.

Integration testing can be performed with the same tools as unit testing. For this reason, newcomers to automated testing are sometimes lured into ignoring the distinction between unit testing and integration testing. Ignoring this distinction is dangerous, because such multipurpose tests often make assumptions about the correctness of some of the units that they involve. This means that the tester loses much of the benefit which automated testing would have granted. We're not aware of the assumptions we make until they bite us, so we need to consciously choose to work in a way that minimizes assumptions. That's one of the reasons why I refer to test-driven development as a *discipline*.

System testing

System testing extends the boundaries of isolation even further, to the point where they don't even exist. System tests check parts of the program, after the whole thing has been plugged together. In a sense, system tests are an extreme form of integration tests.

System tests are very important, but they're not very useful without integration tests and unit tests. You have to be sure of the pieces before you can be sure of the whole. If there's a subtle error somewhere, system testing will tell you that it exists, but not where it is or how to fix it. The odds are good that you've experienced that situation before; it's probably why you hate testing.

You've got Python, right?

This book assumes that you have working knowledge of the Python programming language, and that you have a fully functional Python interpreter available. The assumption is that you have at least version 2.6 of Python, which you can download from `http://www.python.org/`. If you have an earlier version, don't worry: there are sidebars that will help you navigate the differences. You'll also need your favorite text editor.

Summary

In this chapter, we learned what this book is about and what to expect from it. We took a glance at the philosophy of automated testing and test-driven development.

We talked about the different types of tests that combine together to form a complete suite of tests for a program, namely: unit tests, integration tests, and system tests. We learned that unit tests are related to the fundamental components of a program (such as functions), integration tests cover larger swaths of a program (like modules), and system tests encompass testing a program in its entirety.

We learned about how automated testing can help us, by moving the burden of testing mostly onto the computer. You can tell the computer how to check your code, instead of having to do the checks for yourself. That makes it convenient to check your code earlier and more often, saves you from overlooking the things that you would otherwise miss, and helps you quickly locate and fix bugs.

We shed some light on test-driven development, the discipline of writing your tests first, and letting them tell you what needs to be done, in order to write the code you need.

We also discussed the development environment that you'll need, in order to work through this book.

Now that we've learned about the lay of the land (so to speak), we're ready to start writing tests—which is the topic of the next chapter.

2
Doctest: The Easiest Testing Tool

This chapter will introduce you to a fantastic tool called doctest. Doctest is a program that ships with Python that lets you write down what you expect from your code in a way that's easy for both people and computers to read. Doctest files can often be created just by copying the text out of a Python interactive shell and pasting it into a file. Doctest will often be the fastest and easiest way to write tests for your software.

In this chapter, we shall:

◆ Learn the doctest language and syntax

◆ Write doctests embedded in text files

◆ Write doctests embedded in Python docstrings

Basic doctest

Doctest will be the mainstay of your testing toolkit. You'll be using it for tests, of course, but also for things that you may not think of as tests right now. For example, program specifications and API documentation both benefit from being written as doctests and checked alongside your other tests.

Like program source code, doctest tests are written in plain text. Doctest extracts the tests and ignores the rest of the text, which means that the tests can be embedded in human-readable explanations or discussions. This is the feature that makes doctest so suitable for non-classical uses such as program specifications.

Time for action – creating and running your first doctest

We'll create a simple doctest, to demonstrate the fundamentals of using doctest.

1. Open a new text file in your editor, and name it `test.txt`.

2. Insert the following text into the file:

```
This is a simple doctest that checks some of Python's arithmetic
operations.

>>> 2 + 2
4

>>> 3 * 3
10
```

3. We can now run the doctest. The details of how we do that depend on which version of Python we're using. At the command prompt, change to the directory where you saved `test.txt`.

4. If you are using Python 2.6 or higher, type:

```
$ python -m doctest test.txt
```

5. If you are using python 2.5 or lower, the above command may seem to work, but it won't produce the expected result. This is because Python 2.6 is the first version in which doctest looks for test file names on the command line when you invoke it this way.

6. If you're using an older version of Python, you can run your doctest by typing:

```
$ python -c "__import__('doctest').testfile('test.txt')"
```

7. When the test is run, you should see output as shown in the following screen:

```
$ python -m doctest test.txt
*****************************************************************
File "test.txt", line 7, in test.txt
Failed example:
    3 * 3
Expected:
    10
Got:
    9
*****************************************************************
1 items had failures:
    1 of   2 in test.txt
***Test Failed*** 1 failures.
$ 
```

What just happened?

You wrote a doctest file that describes a couple of arithmetic operations, and executed it to check whether Python behaved as the tests said it should. You ran the tests by telling Python to execute doctest on the files that contained the tests.

In this case, Python's behavior differed from the tests because according to the tests, three times three equals ten! However, Python disagrees on that. As doctest expected one thing and Python did something different, doctest presented you with a nice little error report showing where to find the failed test, and how the actual result differed from the expected result. At the bottom of the report, is a summary showing how many tests failed in each file tested, which is helpful when you have more than one file containing tests.

Remember, doctest files are for computer and human consumption. Try to write the test code in a way that human readers can easily understand, and add in plenty of plain language commentary.

The syntax of doctests

You might have guessed from looking at the previous example: doctest recognizes tests by looking for sections of text that look like they've been copied and pasted from a Python interactive session. Anything that can be expressed in Python is valid within a doctest.

Lines that start with a >>> prompt are sent to a Python interpreter. Lines that start with a . . . prompt are sent as continuations of the code from the previous line, allowing you to embed complex block statements into your doctests. Finally, any lines that don't start with >>> or . . ., up to the next blank line or >>> prompt, represent the output expected from the statement. The output appears as it would in an interactive Python session, including both the return value and the one printed to the console. If you don't have any output lines, doctest assumes it to mean that the statement is expected to have no visible result on the console.

Doctest ignores anything in the file that isn't part of a test, which means that you can place explanatory text, HTML, line-art diagrams, or whatever else strikes your fancy in between your tests. We took advantage of that in the previous doctest, to add an explanatory sentence before the test itself.

Time for action – writing a more complex test

We'll write another test (you can add it to `test.txt` if you like) which shows off most of the details of doctest syntax.

1. Insert the following text into your doctest file(`test.txt`), separated from the existing tests by at least one blank line:

```
Now we're going to take some more of doctest's syntax for a spin.

>>> import sys
>>> def test_write():
...         sys.stdout.write("Hello\n")
...         return True
>>> test_write()
Hello
True
```

Think about it for a moment: What does this do? Do you expect the test to pass, or to fail?

2. Run doctest on the test file, just as we discussed before. Because we added the new tests to the same file containing the tests from before, we still see the notification that three times three does not equal ten. Now, though, we also see that five tests were run, which means our new tests ran and succeeded.

```
$ python -m doctest test.txt
**************************************************************
File "test.txt", line 7, in test.txt
Failed example:
    3 * 3
Expected:
    10
Got:
    9
**************************************************************
1 items had failures:
    1 of   5 in test.txt
***Test Failed*** 1 failures.
$ 
```

What just happened?

As far as doctest is concerned, we added three tests to the file.

- The first one says that when we `import sys`, nothing visible should happen.
- The second test says that when we define the `test_write` function, nothing visible should happen.
- The third test says that when we call the `test_write` function, **Hello** and **True** should appear on the console, in that order, on separate lines.

Since all three of these tests pass, doctest doesn't bother to say much about them. All it did was increase the number of tests reported at the bottom from two to five.

Expecting exceptions

That's all well and good for testing that things work as expected, but it is just as important to make sure that things fail when they're supposed to fail. Put another way; sometimes your code is supposed to raise an exception, and you need to be able to write tests that check that behavior as well.

Fortunately, doctest follows nearly the same principle in dealing with exceptions, that it does with everything else; it looks for text that looks like a Python interactive session. That means it looks for text that looks like a Python exception report and traceback, matching it against any exception that gets raised.

Doctest does handle exceptions a little differently from other tools. It doesn't just match the text precisely and report a failure if it doesn't match. Exception tracebacks tend to contain many details that are not relevant to the test, but which can change unexpectedly. Doctest deals with this by ignoring the traceback entirely: it's only concerned with the first line—**Traceback (most recent call last)**—which tells it that you expect an exception, and the part after the traceback, which tells it which exception you expect. Doctest only reports a failure if one of these parts does not match.

That's helpful for a second reason as well: manually figuring out what the traceback would look like, when you're writing your tests would require a significant amount of effort, and would gain you nothing. It's better to simply omit them.

Time for action – expecting an exception

This is yet another test that you can add to `test.txt`, this time testing some code that ought to raise an exception.

1. Insert the following text into your doctest file (Please note that the last line of this text has been wrapped due to the constraints of the book's format, and should be a single line):

```
Here we use doctest's exception syntax to check that Python is
correctly enforcing its grammar.
>>> def faulty():
...     yield 5
...     return 7
Traceback (most recent call last):
SyntaxError: 'return' with argument inside generator
(<doctest test.txt[5]>, line 3)
```

2. The test is supposed to raise an exception, so it will fail if it doesn't raise the exception, or if it raises the wrong exception. Make sure you have your mind wrapped around that: if the test code executes successfully, the test fails, because it expected an exception.

3. Run the tests using doctest and the following screen will be displayed:

```
$ python -m doctest test.txt
********************************************************************
File "test.txt", line 7, in test.txt
Failed example:
    3 * 3
Expected:
    10
Got:
    9
********************************************************************
1 items had failures:
   1 of    6 in test.txt
***Test Failed*** 1 failures.
$
```

What just happened?

Since Python doesn't allow a function to contain both yield statements and return statements with values, having the test to define such a function caused an exception. In this case, the exception was a `SyntaxError` with the expected value. As a result, doctest considered it a match with the expected output, and thus the test passed. When dealing with exceptions, it is often desirable to be able to use a wildcard matching mechanism. Doctest provides this facility through its ellipsis directive, which we'll discuss later.

Expecting blank lines in the output

Doctest uses the first blank line to identify the end of the expected output. So what do you do, when the expected output actually contains a blank line?

Doctest handles this situation by matching a line that contains only the text <BLANKLINE> in the expected output, with a real blank line in the actual output.

Using directives to control doctest

Sometimes, the default behavior of doctest makes writing a particular test inconvenient. That's where doctest directives come to our rescue. Directives are specially formatted comments that you place after the source code of a test, which tell doctest to alter its default behavior in some way.

A directive comment begins with # doctest:, after which comes a comma-separated list of options, that either enable or disable various behaviors. To enable a behavior, write a + (plus symbol) followed by the behavior name. To disable a behavior, white a – (minus symbol) followed by the behavior name.

Ignoring part of the result

It's fairly common that only part of the output of a test is actually relevant to determining whether the test passes. By using the +ELLIPSIS directive, you can make doctest treat the text . . . (called an ellipsis) in the expected output as a wildcard, which will match any text in the output.

When you use an ellipsis, doctest will scan ahead until it finds text matching whatever comes after the ellipsis in the expected output, and continue matching from there. This can lead to surprising results such as an ellipsis matching against a 0-length section of the actual output, or against multiple lines. For this reason, it needs to be used thoughtfully.

Time for action – using ellipsis in tests

We'll use the ellipsis in a few different tests, to get a better feel for what it does and how to use it.

   1.   Insert the following text into your doctest file:

```
Next up, we're exploring the ellipsis.
>>> sys.modules # doctest: +ELLIPSIS
{...'sys': <module 'sys' (built-in)>...}
>>> 'This is an expression that evaluates to a string'
... # doctest: +ELLIPSIS
'This is ... a string'
```

```
>>> 'This is also a string' # doctest: +ELLIPSIS
'This is ... a string'
>>> import datetime
>>> datetime.datetime.now().isoformat() # doctest: +ELLIPSIS
    '...-...-...T...:...:...'
```

2. Run the tests using doctest and the following screen is displayed:.

```
$ python -m doctest test.txt
**********************************************************************
File "test.txt", line 7, in test.txt
Failed example:
    3 * 3
Expected:
    10
Got:
    9
**********************************************************************
1 items had failures:
    1 of   11 in test.txt
***Test Failed*** 1 failures.
$
```

3. None of these tests would pass without the ellipsis. Think about that, and then try making some changes and see if they produce the results you expect.

What just happened?

We just saw how to enable ellipsis matching. In addition, we saw a couple of variations on where the doctest directive comment can be placed, including on a block continuation line by itself.

We got a chance to play with the ellipsis a little bit, and hopefully saw why it should be used carefully. Look at that last test. Can you imagine any output that wasn't an ISO-formatted time stamp, but that it would match anyway?

Ignoring whitespace

Sometimes, whitespace (spaces, tabs, newlines, and their ilk) are more trouble than they're worth. Maybe you want to be able to break a single line of expected output across several lines in your test file, or maybe you're testing a system that uses lots of whitespace but doesn't convey any useful information with it.

Doctest gives you a way to "normalize" whitespace, turning any sequence of whitespace characters, in both the expected output and in the actual output, into a single space. It then checks whether these normalized versions match.

Time for action – normalizing whitespace

We'll write a couple tests that demonstrate how whitespace normalization works.

1. Insert the following text into your doctest file:

```
Next, a demonstration of whitespace normalization.

>>> [1, 2, 3, 4, 5, 6, 7, 8, 9]
... # doctest: +NORMALIZE_WHITESPACE
[1, 2, 3,
 4, 5, 6,
 7, 8, 9]

>>> sys.stdout.write("This text\n contains weird      spacing.")
... # doctest: +NORMALIZE_WHITESPACE
This text contains weird spacing.
```

2. Run the tests using doctest and the following screen is displayed:

```
$ python -m doctest test.txt
**********************************************************************
File "test.txt", line 7, in test.txt
Failed example:
    3 + 3
Expected:
    10
Got:
    9
**********************************************************************
1 items had failures:
    1 of  13 in test.txt
***Test Failed*** 1 failures.
$
```

3. Notice how one of the tests inserts extra whitespace in the expected output, while the other one ignores extra whitespace in the actual output. When you use +NORMALIZE_WHITESPACE, you gain a lot of flexibility with regard to how things are formatted in the text file.

Skipping an example entirely

On some occasions, doctest would recognize some text as an example to be checked, when in truth you want it to be simply text. This situation is rarer than it might at first seem, because usually there's no harm in letting doctest check everything it can. In fact, it is usually helpful to have doctest check everything it can. For those times when you want to limit what doctest checks, though, there's the +SKIP directive.

Time for action – skipping tests

This is an example of how to skip a test:

1. Insert the following text into your doctest file:

    ```
    Now we're telling doctest to skip a test

    >>> 'This test would fail.' # doctest: +SKIP
    If it were allowed to run.
    ```

2. Run the tests using doctest and the following screen will be displayed:

    ```
    $ python -m doctest test.txt
    **********************************************************
    File "test.txt", line 7, in test.txt
    Failed example:
        3 * 3
    Expected:
        10
    Got:
        9
    **********************************************************
    1 items had failures:
        1 of  13 in test.txt
    ***Test Failed*** 1 failures.
    $
    ```

3. Notice that the test didn't fail, and that the number of tests that were run did not change.

What just happened?

The skip directive transformed what would have been a test, into plain text(as far as doctest is concerned). Doctest never ran the test, and in fact never counted it as a test at all.

There are several situations where skipping a test might be a good idea. Sometimes, you have a test which doesn't pass (which you know doesn't pass), but which simply isn't something that should be addressed at the moment. Using the skip directive lets you ignore the test for a while. Sometimes, you have a section of human readable text that looks like a test to the doctest parser, even though it's really only for human consumption. The skip directive can be used to mark that code as not for actual testing.

Other doctest directives

There are a number of other directives that can be issued to adjust the behavior of doctest. They are fully documented at `http://docs.python.org/library/doctest.html#option-flags-and-directives`, but here is a quick overview:

- `+DONT_ACCEPT_TRUE_FOR_1`, which makes doctest treat `True` and `1` as different values, instead of treating them as matching as it normally does.

- `+DONT_ACCEPT_BLANKLINE`, which makes doctest forget about the special meaning of `<BLANKLINE>`.

- `+IGNORE_EXCEPTION_DETAIL`, which makes doctest treat exceptions as matches if the exception type is the same, regardless of whether the rest of the exception matches.

- `+REPORT_UDIFF`, which makes doctest use `unified diff` format when it displays a failed test. This is useful if you are used to reading the `unified diff` format, which is by far the most common diff format within the open source community.

- `+REPORT_CDIFF`, which makes doctest use `context diff` format when it displays a failed test. This is useful if you are used to reading the `context diff` format.

- `+REPORT_NDIFF`, which makes doctest use `ndiff` format when it displays a failed test. This is usefull if you are used to reading the `ndiff` format.

- `+REPORT_ONLY_FIRST_FAILURE` makes doctest avoid printing out failure reports on those tests after it is applied, if a failure report has already been printed. The tests are still executed, and doctest still keeps track of whether they failed or not. Only the report is changed by using this flag.

Execution scope

When doctest is running the tests from text files, all the tests from the same file are run in the same execution scope. That means that if you import a module or bind a variable in one test, that module or variable is still available in later tests. We took advantage of this fact several times in the tests written so far in this chapter: the sys module was only imported once, for example, although it was used in several tests.

That behavior is not necessarily beneficial, because tests need to be isolated from each other. We don't want them to contaminate each other, because if a test depends on something that another test does, or if it fails because of something that another test does, those two tests are in some sense turned into one test that covers a larger section of your code. You don't want that to happen, because knowing which test has failed doesn't give you as much information about what went wrong and where it happened.

So, how can we give each test its own execution scope? There are a few ways to do it. One would be to simply place each test in its own file, along with whatever explanatory text that is needed. This works beautifully, but running the tests can be a pain unless you have a tool to find and run all of them. We'll talk about one such tool (called nose) later.

Another way to give each test its own execution scope, is to define each test within a function, as shown below:

```
>>> def test1():
...     import frob
...     return frob.hash('qux')
>>> test1()
77
```

By doing that, the only thing that ends up in the shared scope is the test function (named `test1` here). The `frob` module, and any other names bound inside the function, are isolated.

The third way is to exercise caution with the names you create, and be sure to set them to known values at the beginning of each test section. In many ways this is the easiest approach, but it's also the one that places the most burden on you, because you have to keep track of what's in the scope.

Why does doctest behave this way, instead of isolating tests from each other? Doctest files are intended not just for computers to read, but also for humans. They often form a sort of narrative, flowing from one thing to the next. It would break the narrative to be constantly repeating what came before. In other words, this approach is a compromise between being a document and being a test framework, a middle ground that works for both humans and computers.

The other framework that we study in depth in this book (called simply unittest) works at a more formal level, and enforces the separation between tests.

Pop quiz – doctest syntax

There is no answer key for these questions. Try your answers in doctest and see if you're right!

1. How does doctest recognize the beginning of a test expression?
2. How does doctest know where the expected output of a text expression begins and ends?
3. How would you tell doctest that you want to break a long expected output across multiple lines, even though that's not how the test actually outputs it?
4. Which parts of an exception report are ignored by doctest?

5. When you bind a variable in a test file, what code can "see" that variable?

6. Why do we care what code can see a variable created by a test?

7. How can we make doctest not care what a section of output contains?

Have a go hero – from English to doctest

Time to stretch your wings a bit! I'm going to give you a description of a single function, in English. Your job is to copy the description into a new text file, and then add tests that describe all the requirements in a way in which the computer can understand and check.

Try to make the doctests that are not just for the computer. Good doctests tend to clarify things for human readers as well. By and large, that means that you present them to human readers as examples interspersed with the text.

Without further ado, here is the English description:

```
The fib(N) function takes a single integer as its only parameter N. If
N is 0 or 1, the function returns 1. If N is less than 0, the function
raises a ValueError. Otherwise, the function returns the sum of fib(N
- 1) and fib(N - 2). The returned value will never be less than 1.
On versions of Python older than 2.2, and if N is at least 52, the
function will raise an OverflowError. A naïve implementation of this
function would get very slow as N increased.
```

I'll give you a hint and point out that the last sentence—about the function being slow—isn't really testable. As computers get faster, any test you write that depends on an arbitrary definition of "slow" will eventually fail. Also, there's no good way to test the difference between a slow function and a function stuck in an infinite loop, so there's no point in trying. If you find yourself needing to do that, it's best to back off and try a different solution.

 Not being able to tell whether a function is stuck or just slow is called the Halting Problem by computer scientists. We know that it can't be solved unless we someday discover a fundamentally better kind of computer. Faster computers won't do the trick, and neither will quantum computers, so don't hold your breath!

Embedding doctests in Python docstrings

Doctests aren't confined to simple text files. You can put doctests into Python's docstrings.

Why would you want to do that? There are a couple of reasons. First of all, docstrings are an important part of the usability of Python code (but only if they tell the truth). If the behavior of a function, method, or module changes and the docstring doesn't get updated, then the docstring becomes misinformation, and a hindrance rather than a help. If the docstring contains a couple of doctest examples, then the out-of-date docstrings can be located automatically. Another reason for placing doctest examples into docstrings is simply that it can be very convenient. This practice keeps the tests, documentation and code all in the same place, where it can all be located easily.

If the docstring becomes home to too many tests, this can destroy its utility as documentation. This should be avoided; if you find yourself with so many tests in the docstrings that they aren't useful as a quick reference, move most of them to a separate file.

Time for action – embedding a doctest in a docstring

We'll embed a test right inside the Python source file that it tests, by placing it inside a docstring.

1. Create a file called `test.py` with the following contents:

```
def testable(x):
    r"""
    The `testable` function returns the square root of its
    parameter, or 3, whichever is larger.
    >>> testable(7)
    3.0
    >>> testable(16)
    4.0
    >>> testable(9)
    3.0
    >>> testable(10) == 10 ** 0.5
    True
    """
    if x < 9:
        return 3.0
    return x ** 0.5
```

2. At the command prompt, change to the directory where you saved `test.py` and then run the tests by typing:

```
$ python -m doctest test.py
```

As mentioned earlier before, if you have an older version of Python, this isn't going to work for you. Instead, you need to type `python -c "__import__('doctest').testmod(__ import__('test'))"`

3. If everything worked, you shouldn't see anything at all. If you want some confirmation that doctest is doing something, turn on verbose reporting by changing the command to:

```
python -m doctest -v test.py
```

For older versions of Python, instead use `python -c "__ import__('doctest').testmod(__import__('test'), verbose=True)"`

What just happened?

You put the doctest right inside the docstring of the function it was testing. This is a good place for tests that also show a user how to do something. It's not a good place for detailed, low-level tests (the above example, which was quite detailed for illustrative purposes, is skirting the edge of being too detailed), because docstrings need to serve as API documentation. You can see the reason for this just by looking back at the example, where the doctests take up most of the room in the docstring, without telling the readers any more than they would have learned from a single test.

Any test that will serve as good API documentation is a good candidate for including in the docstrings.

Notice the use of a raw string for the docstring (denoted by the r character before the first triple-quote). Using raw strings for your docstrings is a good habit to get into, because you usually don't want escape sequences—e.g. \n for newline—to be interpreted by the Python interpreter. You want them to be treated as text, so that they are correctly passed on to doctest.

Doctest directives

Embedded doctests can accept exactly the same directives as doctests in text files can, using exactly the same syntax. Because of this, all of the doctest directives that we discussed before can also be used to affect the way embedded doctests are evaluated.

Execution scope

Doctests embedded in docstrings have a somewhat different execution scope than doctests in text files do. Instead of having a single scope for all of the tests in the file, doctest creates a single scope for each docstring. All of the tests that share a docstring, also share an execution scope, but they're isolated from tests in other docstrings.

The separation of each docstring into its own execution scope often means that we don't need to put much thought into isolating doctests, when they're embedded in docstrings. That is fortunate, since docstrings are primarily intended for documentation, and the tricks needed to isolate the tests might obscure the meaning.

Putting it in practice: an AVL tree

We'll walk step-by-step through the process of using doctest to create a testable specification for a data structure called an AVL Tree. An AVL tree is a way to organize key-value pairs, so that they can be quickly located by key. In other words, it's a lot like Python's built-in dictionary type. The name AVL references the initials of the people who invented this data structure.

As its name suggests, an AVL tree organizes the keys that are stored in it into a tree structure, with each key having up to two **child** keys—one **child** key that is less than the **parent** key by comparison, and one that is more. In the following picture, the key **Elephant** has two child keys, **Goose** has one, and **Aardvark** and **Frog** both have none.

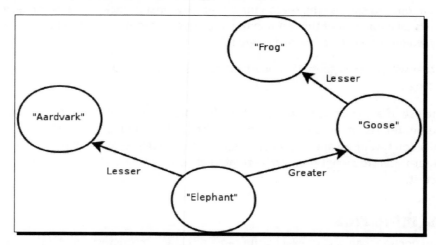

The AVL tree is special, because it keeps one side of the tree from getting much taller than the other, which means that users can expect it to perform reliably and efficiently no matter what. In the previous image, an AVL tree would reorganize to stay balanced if **Frog** gained a child.

We'll write tests for an AVL tree implementation here, rather than writing the implementation itself. Therefore, we'll elaborate over the details of *how* an AVL tree works, in favor of looking at *what* it should do when it works right.

 If you want to know more about AVL Trees, you will find many good references on the Internet. Wikipedia's entry on the subject is a good place to start with: `http://en.wikipedia.org/wiki/AVL_tree`.

We'll start with a plain language specification, and then interject tests between the paragraphs.

 You don't have to actually type all of this into a text file; it is here for you to read and to think about. It's also available in the code download that accompanies this book.

English specification

The first step is to describe what the desired result should be, in normal language. This might be something that you do for yourself, or something that somebody else does for you. If you're working for somebody, hopefully you and your employer can sit down together and work this part out.

In this case, there's not much to work out, because AVL Trees have been fully described for decades. Even so, the description here isn't quite like one you'd find anywhere else. This capacity for ambiguity is exactly the reason why a plain language specification isn't good enough. We need an unambiguous specification, and that's exactly what the tests in a doctest file can give us.

The following text goes in a file called `AVL.txt`, (which you can find in its final form in the accompanying code archive. At this stage of the process, the file contains only the normal language specification.):

> An AVL Tree consists of a collection of nodes organized in a binary tree structure. Each node has left and right children, each of which may be either None or another tree node. Each node has a key, which must be comparable via the less-than operator. Each node has a value. Each node also has a height number, measuring how far the node is from being a leaf of the tree -- a node with height 0 is a leaf.
>
> The binary tree structure is maintained in ordered form, meaning that of a node's two children, the left child has a key that compares less than the node's key and the right child has a key that compares greater than the node's key.

The binary tree structure is maintained in a balanced form, meaning that for any given node, the heights of its children are either the same or only differ by 1.

The node constructor takes either a pair of parameters representing a key and a value, or a dict object representing the key-value pairs with which to initialize a new tree.

The following methods target the node on which they are called, and can be considered part of the internal mechanism of the tree:

Each node has a recalculate_height method, which correctly sets the height number.

Each node has a make_deletable method, which exchanges the positions of the node and one of its leaf descendants, such that the the tree ordering of the nodes remains correct.

Each node has rotate_clockwise and rotate_counterclockwise methods. Rotate_clockwise takes the node's right child and places it where the node was, making the node into the left child of its own former child. Other nodes in the vicinity are moved so as to maintain the tree ordering. The opposite operation is performed by rotate_counterclockwise.

Each node has a locate method, taking a key as a parameter, which searches the node and its descendants for a node with the specified key, and either returns that node or raises a KeyError.

The following methods target the whole tree rooted at the current node. The intent is that they will be called on the root node:

Each node has a get method taking a key as a parameter, which locates the value associated with the specified key and returns it, or raises KeyError if the key is not associated with any value in the tree.

Each node has a set method taking a key and a value as parameters, and associating the key and value within the tree.

Each node has a remove method taking a key as a parameter, and removing the key and its associated value from the tree. It raises KeyError if no values was associated with that key.

Node data

The first three paragraphs of the specification describe the member variables of a AVL tree node, and tell us what the valid values for the variables are. They also tell us how tree height should be measured and define what a balanced tree means. It's our job now to take up those ideas, and encode them into tests that the computer can eventually use to check our code.

We could check these specifications by creating a node and then testing the values, but that would really just be a test of the constructor. It's important to test the constructor, but what we really want to do is to incorporate checks that the node variables are left in a valid state into our tests of each member function.

To that end, we'll define a function that our tests can call to check that the state of a node is valid. We'll define that function just after the third paragraph:

Notice that this test is written as if the AVL tree implementation already existed. It tries to import an `avl_tree` module containing an AVL class, and it tries to use the AVL class is specific ways. Of course, at the moment there is no `avl_tree` module, so the test will fail. That's as it should be. All that the failure means is that, when the time comes to implement the tree, we should do so in a module called `avl_tree`, with contents that function as our test assumes. Part of the benefit of testing like this is being able to test-drive your code before you even write it.

```python
>>> from avl_tree import AVL
>>> def valid_state(node):
...     if node is None:
...         return
...     if node.left is not None:
...         assert isinstance(node.left, AVL)
...         assert node.left.key < node.key
...         left_height = node.left.height + 1
...     else:
...         left_height = 0
...
...     if node.right is not None:
...         assert isinstance(node.right, AVL)
...         assert node.right.key > node.key
...         right_height = node.right.height + 1
...     else:
...         right_height = 0
...
...     assert abs(left_height - right_height) < 2
...     node.key < node.key
...     node.value
>>> def valid_tree(node):
...     if node is None:
...         return
...     valid_state(node)
...     valid_tree(node.left)
...     valid_tree(node.right)
```

Notice that we didn't actually call those functions yet. They aren't tests, per se, but tools that we'll use to simplify writing tests. We define them here, rather than in the Python module that we're going to test, because they aren't conceptually part of the tested code, and because anyone who reads the tests will need to be able to see what the helper functions do.

Constructor

The fourth paragraph describes the constructor for an AVL node: The node constructor takes either a pair of parameters representing a key and a value, or a `dict` object representing the key-value pairs with which to initialize a new tree.

The constructor has two possible modes of operation:

- it can either create a single initialized node
- or it can create and initialize a whole tree of nodes. The test for the single node mode is easy:

```
>>> valid_state(AVL(2, 'Testing is fun'))
```

The other mode of the constructor is a problem, because it is almost certain that it will be implemented by creating an initial tree node and then calling its set method to add the rest of the nodes. Why is that a problem? Because we don't want to test the set method here: this test should be focused entirely on whether the constructor works correctly, *when everything it depends on works*.

 In other words, the tests should be able to assume that everything outside of the specific chunk of code being tested works correctly.

However, that's not always a valid assumption. So, how can we write tests for things that call on code outside of what's being tested?

There is a solution for this problem, about which we'll learn in Chapter 4. For now, we'll just leave the second mode of operation of the constructor untested.

Recalculate height

The `recalculate_height` method is described in the fifth paragraph.

To test it, we'll need a tree for it to operate on, and we don't want to use the second mode of the constructor to create it. After all, that mode isn't tested at all yet, and even if it were, we want this test to be independent of it. We would prefer to make the test entirely independent of the constructor, but in this case we need to make a small exception to the rule(since it's difficult to create an object without calling its constructor in some way).

What we'll do is define a function that builds a specific tree and returns it. This function will be useful in several of our later tests as well. Using this function, testing `recalculate_height` will be easy.

```
>>> def make_test_tree():
...       root = AVL(7, 'seven')
...       root.height = 2
...       root.left = AVL(3, 'three')
...       root.left.height = 1
...       root.left.right = AVL(4, 'four')
...       root.right = AVL(10, 'ten')
...       return root
>>> tree = make_test_tree()
>>> tree.height = 0
>>> tree.recalculate_height()
>>> tree.height
2
```

The `make_test_tree` function builds a tree by manually constructing each part of it and hooking it together into a structure that looks like this:

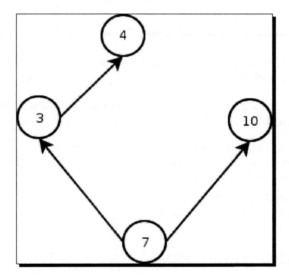

Make deletable

You can't delete a node that has children, because that would leave the node's children disconnected from the rest of the tree. If we delete the **Elephant** node from the bottom of the tree, what do we do about **Aardvark**, **Goose**, and **Frog**? If we delete **Goose**, how do we find **Frog** afterwards?

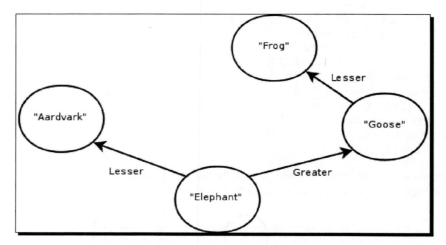

The way around that is to have the node swap places with it's largest leaf descendant on the left side (or its smallest leaf descendant on the right side, but we'll not do it that way).

We'll test this by using the same `make_test_tree` function that we defined before to create a new tree to work on, and then checking that `make_deletable` swaps correctly:

Each node has a make_deletable method, which exchanges the positions of the node and one of its leaf descendants, such that the the tree ordering of the nodes remains correct.

```
>>> tree = make_test_tree()
>>> target = tree.make_deletable()
>>> (tree.value, tree.height)
('four', 2)
>>> (target.value, target.height)
('seven', 0)
```

Something to notice here is that the `make_deletable` function isn't supposed to delete the node that it's called on. It's supposed to move that node into a position where it could be safely deleted. It must do this reorganization of the tree, without violating any of the constraints that define an AVL tree structure.

Rotation

The two rotate functions perform a somewhat tricky manipulation of the links in a tree. You probably found the plain language description of what they do, a bit confusing. This is one of those times when a little bit of code makes a whole lot more sense than any number of sentences.

While tree rotation is usually defined in terms of rearranging the links between nodes in the tree, we'll check whether it worked by looking at the values (rather than by looking directly at the left and right links). This allows the implementation to swap the contents of nodes—rather than the nodes themselves—when it wishes. After all, it's not important to the specification which operation happens, so we shouldn't rule out a perfectly reasonable implementation choice.

The first part of the test code for rotation just creates a tree and verifies that it looks like we expect it to:

```
>>> tree = make_test_tree()
>>> tree.value
'seven'
>>> tree.left.value
'three'
```

Once we have a tree to work with, we try a rotation operation and check that the result still looks like it should:

```
>>> tree.rotate_counterclockwise()
>>> tree.value
'three'
>>> tree.left
None
>>> tree.right.value
'seven'
>>> tree.right.left.value
'four'
>>> tree.right.right.value
'ten'
>>> tree.right.left.value
'four'
>>> tree.left is None
True
```

Finally, we rotate back in the other direction, and check that the final result is the same as the original tree, as we expect it to be:

```
>>> tree.rotate_clockwise()
>>> tree.value
'seven'
>>> tree.left.value
'three'
>>> tree.left.right.value
'four'
>>> tree.right.value
'ten'
>>> tree.right.left is None
True
>>> tree.left.left is None
True
```

Locating a node

The locate method is expected to return a node, or raise a KeyError exception, depending on whether the key exists in the tree or not. We'll use our specially built tree again, so that we know exactly what the tree's structure looks like.

```
>>> tree = make_test_tree()
>>> tree.locate(4).value
'four'
>>> tree.locate(17) # doctest: +ELLIPSIS
Traceback (most recent call last):
KeyError: …
```

The locate method is intended to facilitate insertion, deletion, and lookup of values based on their keys, but it's not a high-level interface. It returns a node object, because it's easy to implement the higher-level operations, if you have a function the finds the right node for you.

Testing the rest of the specification

Like the second mode of the constructor, testing the rest of the specification involves testing code that depends on things outside of itself, which we'll cover in Chapter 4.

Summary

We learned the syntax of doctest, and went through several examples describing how to use it. After that, we took a real-world specification for the AVL tree, and examined how to formalize it as a set of doctests, so that we could use it to automatically check the correctness of an implementation.

Specifically, we covered doctest's default syntax, and the directives that alter it, how to write doctests in text files, how to write doctests in Python docstrings, and what it feels like to use doctest to turn a specification into tests.

Now that we've learned about doctest, we're ready to talk about how to use doctest to do unit testing—which is the topic of the next chapter.

3
Unit Testing with Doctest

Okay, so we've talked about what doctest does, and how to make it behave the way we want. We've talked about testing things with doctest too. What's left to talk about in this chapter, then? In this chapter, we'll be talking about the programming discipline called Unit testing. We'll still be using doctest, but this time the focus is on what you're doing and why, rather than on the details of how to do it.

In this chapter we shall:

- Discuss in detail what Unit testing is
- Talk about the ways in which Unit testing helps various stages of development
- Work with examples that illustrate Unit testing and its advantages

So, let's get on with it!

What is Unit testing and what it is not?

The title of this section, begs another question: "Why do I care?" One answer is that Unit testing is a best practice that has been evolving toward its current form over most of the time that programming has existed. Another answer is that the core principles of Unit testing are just good sense; it might actually be a little embarrassing to our community as a whole that it took us so long to recognize them.

Alright, so what is Unit testing? In its most fundamental form, Unit testing can be defined as testing the smallest meaningful pieces of code (such pieces are called units), in such a way that each piece's success or failure depends only on itself. For the most part, we've been following this principle already.

There's a reason for each part of this definition: we test the smallest meaningful pieces of code because, when a test fails, we want that failure to tell where the problem is us as specifically as possible. We make each test independent because we don't want a test to make any other test succeed, when it should have failed; or fail when it should have succeeded. When tests aren't independent, you can't trust them to tell you what you need to know.

Traditionally, automated testing is associated with Unit testing. Automated testing makes it fast and easy to run unit tests, which tend to be amenable to automation. We'll certainly make heavy use of automated testing with doctest and later with tools such as unittest and Nose as well.

Any test that involves more than one unit is automatically not a unit test. That matters because the results of such tests tend to be confusing. The effects of the different units get tangled together, with the end result that not only do you not know where the problem is (is the mistake in this piece of code, or is it just responding correctly to bad input from some other piece of code?), you're also often unsure exactly what the problem is this output is wrong, but how does each unit contribute to the error? Empirical scientists must perform experiments that check only one hypothesis at a time, whether the subject at hand is chemistry, physics, or the behavior of a body of program code.

Time for action – identifying units

Imagine that you're responsible for testing the following code:

```
class testable:
    def method1(self, number):
        number += 4
        number **= 0.5
        number *= 7
        return number
    def method2(self, number):
        return ((number * 2) ** 1.27) * 0.3
    def method3(self, number):
        return self.method1(number) + self.method2(number)
    def method4(self):
        return 1.713 * self.method3(id(self))
```

1. In this example, what are the units? Is the whole class a single unit, or is each method a separate unit. How about each statement, or each expression? Keep in mind that the definition of a unit is somewhat subjective (although never bigger than a single class), and make your own decision.

2. Think about what you chose. What would the consequences have been if you chose otherwise? For example, if you chose to think of each method as a unit, what would be different if you chose to treat the whole class as a unit?

3. Consider `method4`. Its result depends on all of the other methods working correctly. On top of that, it depends on something that changes from one test run to another, the unique ID of the `self` object. Is it even possible to treat `method4` as a unit in a self-contained test? If we could change anything except `method4`, what would we have to change to enable `method4` to run in a self-contained test and produce a predictable result?

What just happened?

By answering those three questions, you thought about some of the deeper aspects of unit testing.

The question of what constitutes a unit, is fundamental to how you organize your tests. The capabilities of the language affects this choice. C++ and Java make it difficult or impossible to treat methods as units, for example, so in those languages each class is usually treated as a single unit. C, on the other hand, doesn't support classes as language features at all, so the obvious choice of unit is the function. Python is flexible enough that either classes or methods could be considered units, and of course it has stand-alone functions as well, which are also natural to think of as units. Python can't easily handle individual statements within a function or method as units, because they don't exist as separate objects when the test runs. They're all lumped together into a single code object that's part of the function.

The consequences of your choice of unit are far-reaching. The smaller the units are, the more useful the tests tend to be, because they narrow down the location and nature of bugs more quickly. For example, one of the consequences of choosing to treat the testable class as a single unit is that tests of the class will fail if there is a mistake in any of the methods. That tells you that there's a mistake in testable, but not (for example) that it's in `method2`. On the other hand, there is a certain amount of rigmarole involved in treating `method4` and its like as units, to such an extent that the next chapter of the book is dedicated to dealing with such situations. Even so, I recommend using methods and functions as units most of the time, because it pays off in the long run.

In answering the third question, you probably discovered that the functions `id` and `self.method3` would need to have different definitions, definitions that produced a predictable result, and did so without invoking code in any of the other units. In Python, replacing the real function with such stand-ins is fairly easy to do in an ad hoc manner, but we'll be discussing a more structured approach in the next chapter.

Pop quiz – understanding units

Pop quiz – understanding units

Consider this code and then try to answer the questions:

```python
class class_one:
    def __init__(self, arg1, arg2):
        self.arg1 = int(arg1)
        self.arg2 = arg2

    def method1(self, x):
        return x * self.arg1

    def method2(self, x):
        return self.method1(self.arg2) * x
```

1. Assuming that methods are units, how many units exist in the above code?
2. Which units make assumptions about the correct operation of other units? In other words, which units are not independent?
3. What would you need to do to create a test for `method2` that was independent of other units?

Unit testing throughout the development process

We'll walk through the development of a single class, treating it with all the dignity of a real project. We'll be strictly careful to integrate unit testing into every phase of the project. This may seem silly at times, but just play along. There's a lot to learn from the experience.

The example we'll be working with is a PID controller. The basic idea is that a PID controller is a feedback loop for controlling some piece of real-world hardware. It takes input from a sensor that can measure some property of the hardware, and generates a control signal that adjusts that property toward some desired state. The position of a robot arm in a factory might be controlled by a PID controller.

 If you want to know more about PID controllers, the Internet is rife with information. The Wikipedia entry is a good place to start: http://en.wikipedia.org/wiki/PID_controller.

Design phase

Our notional client comes to us with the following (rather sparse) specification:

> We want a class that implements a PID controller for a single variable. The measurement, setpoint, and output should all be real numbers.

> We need to be able to adjust the setpoint at runtime, but we want it to have a memory, so that we can easily return to the previous setpoint.

Time for action – unit testing during design

Time to make that specification a bit more formal—and complete—by writing unit tests that describe the desired behavior.

1. We need to write a test that describes the PID constructor. After checking our references, we determine that a PID controller is defined by three `gains`, and a `setpoint`. The controller has three components: proportional, integral and derivative (hence the name PID). Each `gain` is a number that determines how much one of the three parts of the controller has on the final result. The `setpoint` determines what the goal of the controller is; in other words, to where it's trying to move the controlled variable. Looking at all that, we decide that the constructor should just store the `gains` and the `setpoint`, along with initializing some internal state that we know we'll need due to reading up on the workings of a PID controller:

```
>>> import pid

>>> controller = pid.PID(P=0.5, I=0.5, D=0.5, setpoint=0)

>>> controller.gains
(0.5, 0.5, 0.5)
>>> controller.setpoint
[0.0]
>>> controller.previous_time is None
True
>>> controller.previous_error
0.0
>>> controller.integrated_error
0.0
```

2. We need to write tests that describe measurement processing. This is the controller in action, taking a measured value as its input and producing a control signal that should smoothly move the measured variable to the setpoint. For this to work correctly, we need to be able to control what the controller sees as the current time. After that, we plug our test input values into the math that defines a PID controller, along with the gains, to figure out what the correct outputs would be:

```
>>> import time
>>> real_time = time.time
>>> time.time = (float(x) for x in xrange(1, 1000)).next
>>> pid = reload(pid)
>>> controller = pid.PID(P=0.5, I=0.5, D=0.5, setpoint=0)
>>> controller.measure(12)
-6.0
>>> controller.measure(6)
-3.0
>>> controller.measure(3)
-4.5
>>> controller.measure(-1.5)
-0.75
>>> controller.measure(-2.25)
-1.125
>>> time.time = real_time
```

3. We need to write tests that describe setpoint handling. Our client asked for a setpoint stack, so we write tests that check such stack behavior. Writing code that uses this stack behavior brings to our attention that fact that a PID controller with no setpoint is not a meaningful entity, so we add a test that checks that the PID class rejects that situation by raising an exception.

```
>>> pid = reload(pid)
>>> controller = pid.PID(P = 0.5, I = 0.5, D = 0.5, setpoint = 0)
>>> controller.push_setpoint(7)
>>> controller.setpoint
[0.0, 7.0]
>>> controller.push_setpoint(8.5)
>>> controller.setpoint
[0.0, 7.0, 8.5]
>>> controller.pop_setpoint()
8.5
>>> controller.setpoint
```

```
[0.0, 7.0]

>>> controller.pop_setpoint()
7.0
>>> controller.setpoint
[0.0]

>>> controller.pop_setpoint()
Traceback (most recent call last):
ValueError: PID controller must have a setpoint
```

What just happened?

Our clients gave us a pretty good initial specification, but it left a lot of details to assumption. By writing these tests, we've codified exactly what our goal is. Writing the tests forced us to make our assumptions explicit. Additionally, we've gotten a chance to use the object, which gives us an understanding of it that would otherwise be hard to get at this stage.

Normally we'd place the doctests in the same file as the specification, and in fact that's what you'll find in the book's code archive. In the book format, we used the specification text as the description for each step of the example.

You could ask how many tests we should write for each piece of the specification. After all, each test is for certain specific input values, so when code passes it, all it proves is that the code produces the right results for that specific input. The code could conceivably do something entirely wrong, and still pass the test. The fact is that it's usually a safe assumption that the code you'll be testing was supposed to do the right thing, and so a single test for each specified property fairly well distinguishes between working and non-working code. Add to that tests for any boundaries specified—for "The X input may be between the values 1 and 7, inclusive" you might add tests for X values of 0.9 and 7.1 to make sure they weren't accepted—and you're doing fine.

There were a couple of tricks we pulled to make the tests repeatable and independent. In every test after the first, we called the reload function on the pid module, to reload it from the disk. That has the effect of resetting anything that might have changed in the module, and causes it to re-import any modules that it depends on. That latter effect is particularly important, since in the tests of measure, we replaced time.time with a dummy function. We want to be sure that the pid module uses the dummy time function, so we reload the pid module. If the real time function is used instead of the dummy, the test won't be useful, because there will be only one time in all of history at which it would succeed. Tests need to be repeatable.

The dummy time function is created by making an iterator that counts through the integers from 1 to 999 (as floating point values), and binding `time.time` to that iterator's `next` method. Once we were done with the time-dependent tests, we replaced the original `time.time`.

Right now, we have tests for a module that doesn't exist. That's good! Writing the tests was easier than writing the module will be, and it gives us a stepping stone toward getting the module right, quickly and easily. As a general rule, you always want to have tests ready before the code that they test is written.

Pop quiz – unit testing during design

1. Why should we care whether tests are independent of each other, when the code they're testing is imaginary and the tests can't even be run?

2. Why are you, as a programmer, writing tests during this phase? Should this be part of the job of the people writing the specification instead?

3. Tests at this phase try to make use of code that hasn't been written yet, and so they end up—in a sense—defining that code. What advantages and disadvantages does this have?

Have a go hero

Try this a few times on your own: Describe some program or module that you'd enjoy having access to in real life, using normal language. Then go back through it and try writing tests, describing the program or module. Keep an eye out for places where writing the test makes you aware of ambiguities in your prior description, or makes you realize that there's a better way to do something.

Development phase

With tests in hand, we're ready to write some code. The tests will act as a guide to us, a specification that actively tells us when we get something wrong.

Time for action – unit testing during development

1. The first step is to run the tests. Of course, we have a pretty good idea of what's going to happen; they're all going to fail. Still, it's useful to know exactly what the failures are, because those are the things that we need to address by writing code.

```
$ python -m doctest pid.txt
**********************************************************************
File "pid.txt", line 5, in pid.txt
Failed example:
    import pid
Exception raised:
    Traceback (most recent call last):
      File "/usr/lib64/python2.6/doctest.py", line 1231, in __run
        compileflags, 1) in test.globs
      File "<doctest pid.txt[0]>", line 1, in <module>
        import pid
    ImportError: No module named pid
```

There are many more failing tests after that, but you get the idea.

2. Taking our cue from the tests, and our references on PID controllers, we write the
pid.py module:

```
from time import time

class PID:
    def __init__(self, P, I, D, setpoint):
        self.gains = (float(P), float(I), float(D))
        self.setpoint = [float(setpoint)]
        self.previous_time = None
        self.previous_error = 0.0
        self.integrated_error = 0.0

    def push_setpoint(self, target):
        self.setpoint.append(float(target))

    def pop_setpoint(self):
        if len(self.setpoint) > 1:
            return self.setpoint.pop()
        raise ValueError('PID controller must have a setpoint')

    def measure(self, value):
        now = time()
        P, I, D = self.gains

        err = value - self.setpoint[-1]

        result = P * err
        if self.previous_time is not None:
            delta = now - self.previous_time
            self.integrated_error +q= err * delta
            result += I * self.integrated_error
            result += D * (err - self.previous_error) / delta
        self.previous_error = err
        self.previous_time = now

        return result
```

3. Next we run the tests again. We're hoping that they will all pass, but unfortunately the measure method seems to have some sort of bug.

```
$ python -m doctest pid.txt
**********************************************************************
File "pid.txt", line 24, in pid.txt
Failed example:
    controller.measure(12)
Expected:
    -6.0
Got:
    6.0
**********************************************************************
File "pid.txt", line 26, in pid.txt
Failed example:
    controller.measure(6)
Expected:
    -3.0
Got:
    3.0
```

There are several more reports showing similar things (five tests in total should fail). The measure function is working backwards, returning positive numbers when it should be returning negative, and vice-versa.

4. We know we need to look for a sign error in the measure method, so we don't have too much trouble finding and fixing the bug. The measured value should be subtracted from the setpoint, not the other way around, on the fourth line of the measure method:

```
err = self.setpoint[-1] - value
```

After fixing that, we find that all the tests pass.

What just happened?

We used our tests to tell us what needed to be done and when our code was finished. Our first run of the tests gave us a list of things that needed to be written; a to-do list, of sorts. After we wrote some code, we ran the tests again to see if it was doing what we expected, which gave us a new to-do list. We keep on alternating between running the tests and writing code until the tests all passed. When all the tests pass, either we're done, or we need to write more tests.

Whenever we find a bug that isn't already caught by a test, the right thing to do is to add a test that catches it, and then to fix it. That way, you not only have a fixed bug, you have a test that covers some aspect of the program that wasn't tested before. That test may well catch other bugs in the future, or tell you if you accidentally re-introduced the original bug.

This "test a little, code a little" style of programming is called *Test-Driven Development*, and you'll find that it's very productive.

Notice that the pattern in the way the tests failed was immediately apparent. There's no guarantee that this will always be the case, of course, but it's quite common. Combined with the ability to narrow your attention to the specific units that are having problems, debugging is usually a snap.

Another thing to think about is test isolation. The methods of the `PID` class make use of variables stored in `self`, which means that in order for the tests to be isolated, we have to make sure that none of the changes to `self` variables made by any method propagate to any other method. We did that by just reloading the `pid` module and making a new instance of the `PID` class for each test. As long as the test (and the code being tested) doesn't invoke any other methods on `self`, that's all that we need.

Feedback phase

So, we have a PID controller, and it passes all the tests. We're feeling pretty good. Time to brave the lions, and show it to the client!

Luckily for us, for the most part they like it. They do have a few requests, though: They want us to let them optionally specify the current time as a parameter to `measure`, instead of just using `time.time` to figure it out. They also want us to change the signature of the constructor so that it takes an initial measurement and optional time as parameters. Finally, they want us to rename the `measure` function to `calculate_response`, because they think that more clearly describes what it does.

Time for action – unit testing during feedback

So, how are we going to deal with this? The program passes all the tests, but the tests no longer reflect the requirements.

1. Add the initial parameter to the constructor test, and update the expected results.

2. Add a second constructor test, which tests the optional time parameter that is now expected to be part of the constructor.

3. Change the `measure` method's name to `calculate_response` in all tests.

4. Add the initial constructor parameter in the `calculate_response` test – while we're doing that, we notice that this is going to change the way the `calculate_response` function behaves. We contact the client for clarification, and they decide it's okay, so we update the expectations to match what we calculate should happen after the change.

5. Add a second `calculate_response` test, which checks its behavior when the optional time parameter is supplied.

6. After making all those changes, our specification/test file looks like the following. Lines that have been changed or added are formatted differently, to help you spot them more easily.

We want a class that implements a PID controller for a single variable. The measurement, setpoint, and output should all be real numbers. The constructor should accept an initial measurement value in addition to the gains and setpoint.

```
>>> import time
>>> real_time = time.time
>>> time.time = (float(x) for x in xrange(1, 1000)).next
>>> import pid
>>> controller = pid.PID(P=0.5, I=0.5, D=0.5, setpoint=0,
...                       initial=12)
>>> controller.gains
(0.5, 0.5, 0.5)
>>> controller.setpoint
[0.0]
>>> controller.previous_time
1.0
>>> controller.previous_error
-12.0
>>> controller.integrated_error
0.0
>>> time.time = real_time
```

The constructor should also optionally accept a parameter specifying when the initial measurement was taken.

```
>>> pid = reload(pid)
>>> controller = pid.PID(P=0.5, I=0.5, D=0.5, setpoint=1,
...                       initial=12, when=43)
>>> controller.gains
(0.5, 0.5, 0.5)
>>> controller.setpoint
[1.0]
>>> controller.previous_time
43.0
>>> controller.previous_error
-11.0
```

```
>>> controller.integrated_error
0.0

>>> real_time = time.time
>>> time.time = (float(x) for x in xrange(1, 1000)).next
>>> pid = reload(pid)
>>> controller = pid.PID(P=0.5, I=0.5, D=0.5, setpoint=0,
...                      initial=12)
>>> controller.calculate_response(6)
-3.0
>>> controller.calculate_response(3)
-4.5
>>> controller.calculate_response(-1.5)
-0.75
>>> controller.calculate_response(-2.25)
-1.125
>>> time.time = real_time
```

The calculate_response method should be willing to accept a parameter specifying at what time the call is happening.

```
>>> pid = reload(pid)
>>> controller = pid.PID(P=0.5, I=0.5, D=0.5, setpoint=0,
...                      initial=12, when=1)
>>> controller.calculate_response(6, 2)
-3.0
>>> controller.calculate_response(3, 3)
-4.5
>>> controller.calculate_response(-1.5, 4)
-0.75
>>> controller.calculate_response(-2.25, 5)
-1.125
```

We need to be able to adjust the setpoint at runtime, but we want it to have a memory, so that we can easily return to the previous setpoint.

```
>>> pid = reload(pid)
>>> controller = pid.PID(P=0.5, I=0.5, D=0.5, setpoint=0,
...                      initial=12)
>>> controller.push_setpoint(7)
>>> controller.setpoint
[0.0, 7.0]
>>> controller.push_setpoint(8.5)
```

```
>>> controller.setpoint
[0.0, 7.0, 8.5]
>>> controller.pop_setpoint()
8.5
>>> controller.setpoint
[0.0, 7.0]
>>> controller.pop_setpoint()
7.0
>>> controller.setpoint
[0.0]
>>> controller.pop_setpoint()
Traceback (most recent call last):
ValueError: PID controller must have a setpoint
```

What just happened?

Our tests didn't match the requirements any more, so they had to change.

Well and good, but we don't want them to change too much, because our collection of tests helps us avoid regressions in our code. Regressions are changes that cause something that used to work, to stop working. One of the best ways to avoid them is to avoid deleting tests. If you still have tests in place that check for every desired behavior and every bug fixed, then if you introduce a regression you find out about it immediately.

That's one reason why we added new tests to check the behavior when the optional time parameters are supplied. The other reason is that if we added those parameters to the existing tests, we wouldn't have any tests of what happens when you don't use those parameters. We always want to check every code path through each unit.

Sometimes, a test just isn't right any more. For example, tests that make use of the `measure` method are just plain wrong, and need to be updated to call `calculate_response` instead. When we change these tests, though, we still change them as little as possible. After all, we don't want the test to stop checking for old behavior that's still correct, and we don't want to introduce a bug in the test itself.

The addition of the `initial` parameter to the constructor is a big deal. It not only changes the way the constructor should behave, it also changes the way the `calculate_response` (née `measure`) method should behave in a rather dramatic way. Since this is a change in the correct behavior (a fact which we didn't realize until the tests pointed it out to us, which in turn allowed us to get confirmation of what the correct behavior should be from our clients *before* we started writing the code), we have no choice but to go through and change the tests, recalculating the expected outputs. However, doing all that work has a benefit over and above the future ability to check that the function is working correctly; it makes it much easier to comprehend how the function should work when we actually write it.

Back to the development phase

Well, it's time to go back into development. In real life, there's no telling how often we'd have to cycle back and forth between development and feedback, but we would want to keep the cycle short. The more often we switch back and forth, the more in contact we are with what our clients really want, and that makes for a more productive, more rewarding job.

Time for action – unit testing during development... again

We've got our updated tests, so now it's time to get back into a state where all of our tests pass.

1. First off, let's run the tests, and so get a new list of things that need to be done.

```
$ python -m doctest pid.txt
**********************************************************************
File "pid.txt", line 10, in pid.txt
Failed example:
    controller = pid.PID(P = 0.5, I = 0.5, D = 0.5, setpoint = 0,
                         initial = 12)
Exception raised:
    Traceback (most recent call last):
      File "/usr/lib64/python2.6/doctest.py", line 1231, in __run
        compileflags, 1) in test.globs
      File "<doctest pid.txt[4]>", line 2, in <module>
        initial = 12)
    TypeError: __init__() got an unexpected keyword argument 'initial'
```

There are several more error reports after this, of course. Doctest reports a total of 32 failing examples, although that's not particularly meaningful since none of the tests are able to even construct a PID object right now. Fixing that constructor would be a reasonable place to start.

2. Using the doctest report as a guide, we set about adjusting the PID class. This is going to work best as an iterative process, where we make a few changes, then run the tests, then make a few changes, and so on. In the end, though, we'll end up with something like the following (the `push_setpoint` and `pop_setpoint` methods are unchanged, so they've been omitted here to save space):

```
from time import time

class PID:
    def __init__(self, P, I, D, setpoint, initial, when=None):
        self.gains = (float(P), float(I), float(D))
        self.setpoint = [float(setpoint)]

        if when is None:
```

```
            self.previous_time = time()
        else:
            self.previous_time = float(when)
        self.previous_error = self.setpoint[-1] - float(initial)
        self.integrated_error = 0.0
    def calculate_response(self, value, now=None):
        if now is None:
            now = time()
        else:
            now = float(now)
        P, I, D = self.gains
        err = self.setpoint[-1] - value
        result = P * err
        delta = now - self.previous_time
        self.integrated_error += err * delta
        result += I * self.integrated_error
        result += D * (err - self.previous_error) / delta

        self.previous_error = err
        self.previous_time = now

        return result
```

We check the tests again, and they all pass.

What just happened?

This wasn't very different from our first time through the development phase. Just as before, we had a set of tests, and the error report from those tests gives us a checklist of things we need to fix. As we work, we keep an eye out for things that need to be tested, but aren't yet, and add those tests. When all the tests pass, we check with our client again (which means we go back to the feedback phase). Eventually the client will be satisfied. Then we can move on to releasing the code, and then into the maintenance phase.

As we're working, the tests give us a nice, fast way to get a sense of whether what we're doing works, and how far along we are. It makes it easy for us to see that the code we're writing does something, which in turn makes the coding process flow better, and even makes it more fun. Writing code that just sits there is boring and bug-prone, but because we have the tests, our code doesn't just sit there. It's active, and we can see the results at any time.

Maintenance phase

Now that we've passed on our work to our client, we have to make sure that they stay happy with it. That means fixing any bugs that may have slipped past our tests (hopefully not many) and making small improvements on request.

Time for action – unit testing during maintenance

Our client has come to us with a change request: they don't want the PID class to accept negative gain values in its constructor, because negative gains make its output push things further away from the setpoint, instead of pulling them toward it.

1. We add new tests that describe what should happen when negative gains are passed to the constructor. We're testing something that the old tests don't describe, so we get to leave the old tests alone and just add new tests. That's a good thing, because it means that the old tests will be certain to catch any regressions that we might introduce while we're working on this.

   It's important that the P, I and D gains not be negative.

   ```
   >>> pid = reload(pid)
   >>> controller = pid.PID(P=-0.5, I=0.5, D=0.5, setpoint=0,
   ...                      initial=12)
   Traceback (most recent call last):
   ValueError: PID controller gains must be non-negative

   >>> pid = reload(pid)
   >>> controller = pid.PID(P=0.5, I=-0.5, D=0.5, setpoint=0,
   ...                      initial=12)
   Traceback (most recent call last):
   ValueError: PID controller gains must be non-negative

   >>> pid = reload(pid)
   >>> controller = pid.PID(P=0.5, I=0.5, D=-0.5, setpoint=0,
   ...                      initial=12)
   Traceback (most recent call last):
   ValueError: PID controller gains must be non-negative
   ```

2. Run the tests to see what needs doing. As we might expect in this case, doctest reports three failures, one for each of the tests we just added – The `PID` class didn't raise the expected `ValueErrors`.

```
$ python -m doctest pid.txt
**********************************************************************
File "pid.txt", line 100, in pid.txt
Failed example:
    controller = pid.PID(P = -0.5, I = 0.5, D = 0.5, setpoint = 0,
                         initial = 12)
Expected:
    Traceback (most recent call last):
    ValueError: PID controller gains must be non-negative
Got nothing
**********************************************************************
File "pid.txt", line 106, in pid.txt
Failed example:
    controller = pid.PID(P = 0.5, I = -0.5, D = 0.5, setpoint = 0,
                         initial = 12)
Expected:
    Traceback (most recent call last):
    ValueError: PID controller gains must be non-negative
Got nothing
**********************************************************************
File "pid.txt", line 112, in pid.txt
Failed example:
    controller = pid.PID(P = 0.5, I = 0.5, D = -0.5, setpoint = 0,
                         initial = 12)
Expected:
    Traceback (most recent call last):
    ValueError: PID controller gains must be non-negative
Got nothing
**********************************************************************
1 items had failures:
   3 of  51 in pid.txt
***Test Failed*** 3 failures.
```

3. Now we write the code that will make the `PID` class pass the tests. That's easily done by adding the following to the constructor:

```
if P < 0 or I < 0 or D < 0:
    raise ValueError('PID controller gains must be non-negative')
```

4. We run the tests again, and when they all pass, we can report to our client that the change has been implemented.

 Remember, if doctest doesn't print anything, then all the tests passed. It only tells you about errors, unless you pass `-v` on its command line.

What just happened?

That looked pretty straightforward, but the fact is that our body of tests was a big help to us here. When we're mucking around in a codebase, trying to update its behavior, or to fix a bug that we've never even considered might exist, it's easy to break other parts of the program. This is doubly so when the codebase is one that we haven't worked with for a while, as is often the case with maintenance requests. Thanks to the expertise stored in the tests that we wrote, we don't have to worry about forgetting details of what constitutes correct behavior, or what might go wrong in various parts of the code. We don't have to waste time or effort re-learning those details when we come back to the code. Instead, we can just execute the tests.

Our clients don't necessarily know about our testing process, but they appreciate the fast turnaround time we can give them because of it.

Reuse phase

Eventually, there comes a time when—if the code we wrote is useful—we'll want to use it again in a different project. That means we're going to be putting it in a context where the assumptions made in the code may no longer be valid.

Time for action – unit testing during reuse

Our client wants to use a PID controller in a new project, but there's a twist: The value that's going to be measured and controlled is represented as a complex number. When we wrote the PID controller, there was an implicit assumption that the values would always be representable as floating point numbers. What do we have to do to re-use this code? Let's find out.

 By the way, if you don't know what complex numbers are, don't worry. They're not actually complicated; a complex number is just a pair of coordinates, much like latitude and longitude.

1. Write some tests that use complex numbers for `setpoint`, `initial` and the measurements. Since we want to make sure we don't break code that still uses floating point numbers, we don't replace the older tests, we just add more.

You'll notice that we're using some very random-looking numbers here. They're not random at all. Complex numbers can be thought of as representing coordinates; they represent the same values that we used in our earlier tests, except rotated 45 degrees and translated by `1+1j`. For example, where before we used the value `12`, we now use the value of `12 * complex(cos(0.25 * pi), sin(0.25 * pi))+ (1+1j)`, which is `9.4852813742385 695+9.4852813742385695j`. If you don't understand, or don't care, it's enough to know that the same expression can be used to calculate the value of every complex number in this example: just substitute the appropriate number in place of the `12`. You can find `sin`, `cos` and `pi` in the `math` module.

(Some of the input lines here are very long, and have to be wrapped to fit onto the page. They shouldn't be wrapped in the doctest file.)

```
We want to be able to use complex numbers as the measurement and
setpoint for the PID controller.

>>> pid = reload(pid)
>>> controller = pid.PID(P=0.5, I=0.5, D=0.5,
...        setpoint = 1 + 1j,
...        initial = 9.4852813742385695+9.4852813742385695j,
...        when = 1)
>>> controller.calculate_response(5.2426406871192848+5.24264068711
92848j, 2)
(-2.1213203435596424-2.1213203435596424j)

>>> controller.calculate_response(3.1213203435596424+3.12132034355
96424j, 3)
(-3.1819805153394638-3.1819805153394638j)

>>> controller.calculate_response(-0.060660171779821193-
0.060660171779821193j, 4)
(-0.53033008588991093-0.53033008588991093j)

>>> controller.calculate_response(-0.5909902576697319-
0.5909902576697319j, 5)
(-0.79549512883486606-0.79549512883486606j)
```

2. Okay, the correct behavior has been calculated and the tests have been written. Let's run them and see what doesn't work. We run the doctests, and the first thing that comes out of it is an exception raised in the constructor. It looks like our floating point assumption is already causing trouble. There are several more error reports after this, but since the constructor didn't work, we can't expect them to make much sense.

```
$ python -m doctest pid.txt
******************************************************************
File "pid.txt", line 121, in pid.txt
Failed example:
    controller = pid.PID(P = 0.5, I = 0.5, D = 0.5,
        setpoint = 1 + 1j,
        initial = 9.4852813742385695+9.4852813742385695j, when = 1)
Exception raised:
    Traceback (most recent call last):
      File "/usr/lib64/python2.6/doctest.py", line 1231, in __run
        compileflags, 1) in test.globs
      File "<doctest pid.txt[52]>", line 3, in <module>
        initial = 9.4852813742385695+9.4852813742385695j, when = 1)
      File "pid.py", line 10, in __init__
        self.setpoint = [float(setpoint)]
    TypeError: can't convert complex to float; use abs(z)
```

3. The problems in the constructor arise from passing complex numbers into the constructor for the `float` class, which is not allowed. Do we really need to call `float` there? Sometimes we do, because we don't want to use integers for `setpoint` and `initial`. Integer division doesn't work the same way as floating point division in versions of Python less than 3.0, so integers could severely mess up the behavior of the system.

So, we want to call the `float` constructor on `initial` and `setpoint`, *unless* they are complex numbers. That makes the constructor look like this (again, watch out for the wrapping of long lines):

```python
def __init__(self, P, I, D, setpoint, initial, when=None):
    self.gains = (float(P), float(I), float(D))

    if P < 0 or I < 0 or D < 0:
        raise ValueError('PID controller gains must be
non-negative')

    if not isinstance(setpoint, complex):
        setpoint = float(setpoint)

    if not isinstance(initial, complex):
        initial = float(initial)

    self.setpoint = [setpoint]

    if when is None:
        self.previous_time = time()
    else:
        self.previous_time = float(when)

    self.previous_error = self.setpoint[-1] - initial
    self.integrated_error = 0.0
```

4. Okay, we've fixed the constructor. We run the tests again, and all the tests pass! Somewhat surprisingly, perhaps, the `calculate_response` function is already compatible with complex numbers.

What just happened?

Writing our tests originally helped us to determine what assumptions we were making, and the tests check those assumptions explicitly. Furthermore, even the assumptions that we didn't know we were making have a tendency to be checked by our tests, because they are implicit in our expectations. An example of this is the floating point results that the tests expected. If we had just removed the calls to float in the constructor entirely, all of those tests that were expecting a float would have failed, telling us that we'd violated an implicit assumption about the behavior of the code.

Our tests give us confidence that our code is correct (even when its operating on complex numbers), and that we haven't broken anything else by changing the code. No muss, no fuss; it works. If one of the tests had failed, that would have told us where the problems lay. Either way, we know where we are in the project and what needs to be done next, which lets us keep the process rolling along.

Pop quiz – unit testing

1. When you write a test, should you do it while referring to the code being tested, or should you do it based on your expectations of what correct behavior should be, before the code is even written?

2. True or false: You should avoid changing or deleting tests whenever possible, and prefer changing them to deleting them when you aren't able to keep them untouched.

3. How often do you think your tests should be run? Can you think of any particularly good times to execute the tests?

4. If your development process is test driven, you as a programmer will spend most of your time doing what?

Have a go hero – test-driven development

Try using the methods that we've talked about in this chapter to implement this plain language specification:

```
The library consists of three classes, one representing bank accounts,
one representing people, and one representing monetary transactions.
Person objects should be able to draw on zero or more accounts,
and account objects should be accessible to one or more people.
Transactions should represent the transfer of a certain amount of
money between one person and another, by transferring the money from
an account accessible by the first person to an account accessible by
the second.
Attempts to create invalid transactions should fail.
After having been created, it should be possible to execute a
transaction to perform the actual transfer between accounts.
All monies should be represented as fixed point numbers, not floating
point.
```

Summary

We learned a lot in this chapter about Unit testing and Test-Driven Development, which are best-practice disciplines for quickly building reliable programs.

Specifically, we covered the definition of Unit testing, how unit testing can help during each stage of the development process, what it feels like to use unit testing to drive development, and how it can make the process quicker and more pleasant.

Now that we've learned about Unit testing, we're ready to talk about making it easier to isolate tests with the help of mock objects—which is the topic of the next chapter.

4

Breaking Tight Coupling by using Mock Objects

Several times in the previous chapters, we've run across cases where we needed to go out of our way to make sure that units didn't contaminate each others' tests. Now we're going to look at a formalization of how to handle those situations—mock objects—and also at a specific mock object toolkit called Python Mocker.

In this chapter, we shall:

- ◆ Examine the ideas of mock objects in general
- ◆ Learn how to use Python Mocker
- ◆ Learn how to mock the "self" parameter of a method

So let's get on with it!

Installing Python Mocker

For the first time, we're using a tool that isn't included in the standard Python distribution. That means that we need to download and install it.

Time for action – installing Python Mocker

1. At the time of this writing, Python Mocker's home page is located at `http://labix.org/mocker`, while its downloads are hosted at `https://launchpad.net/mocker/+download`. Go ahead and download the newest version, and we'll see about installing it.

2. The first thing that needs to be done is to unzip the downloaded file. It's a `.tar.bz2`, which should just work for Unix, Linux, or OSX users. Windows users will need a third-party program (7-Zip works well: `http://www.7-zip.org/`) to uncompress the archive. Store the uncompressed file in some temporary location.

3. Once you have the files unzipped somewhere, go to that location via the command line. Now, to do this next step, you either need to be allowed to write files into your Python installation's site-packages directory (which you are, if you're the one who installed Python in the first place) or you need to be using Python version 2.6 or higher.

4. If you can write to site-packages, type

    ```
    $ python setup.py install
    ```

5. If you can't write to site-packages, but you're using Python 2.6 or higher, type

    ```
    $ python setup.py install --user
    ```

Sometimes, a tool called `easy_install` can simplify the installation process of Python modules and packages. If you want to give it a try, download and install `setuptools` from `http://pypi.python.org/pypi/setuptools`, according to the directions on that page, and then run the command `easy_install mocker`. Once that command is done, you should be ready to use Nose.

Once you have successfully run the installer, Python Mocker is ready for use.

The idea of a mock object

"Mock" in this sense means "imitation," and that's exactly what a mock object does. Mock objects imitate the real objects that make up your program, without actually being those objects or relying on them in any way.

Instead of doing whatever the real object would do, a mock object performs predefined simple operations that *look like what the real object should do*. That means its methods return appropriate values (which you told it to return) or raise appropriate exceptions (which you told it to raise). A mock object is like a mockingbird; imitating the calls of other birds without comprehending them.

We've already used one mock object in our earlier work when we replaced `time.time` with an object (in Python, functions are objects) that returned an increasing series of numbers. The mock object was like `time.time`, except that it always returned the same series of numbers, no matter when we ran our test or how fast the computer was that we ran it on. In other words, it decoupled our test from an external variable.

That's what mock objects are all about: decoupling tests from external variables. Sometimes those variables are things like the external time or processor speed, but usually the variables are the behavior of other units.

Python Mocker

The idea is pretty straightforward, but one look at that mock version of `time.time` from the previous chapter shows that creating mock objects without using a toolkit of some sort can be a dense and annoying process, and can interfere with the readability of your tests. This is where Python Mocker (or any of several other mock object toolkits, depending on preference) comes in.

Time for action – exploring the basics of Mocker

We'll walk through some of the simplest—and most useful—features of Mocker. To do that, we'll write tests that describe a class representing a specific mathematical operation (multiplication) which can be applied to the values of arbitrary other mathematical operation objects. In other words, we'll work on the guts of a spreadsheet program (or something similar).

We're going to use Mocker to create mock objects to stand in place of the real operation objects.

1. Create up a text file to hold the tests, and add the following at the beginning (assuming that all the mathematical operations will be defined in a module called `operations`):

    ```
    >>> from mocker import Mocker
    >>> import operations
    ```

2. We've decided that every mathematical operation class should have a constructor accepting the objects representing the new object's operands. It should also have an evaluate function that accepts a dictionary of variable bindings as its parameter and returns a number as the result. We can write the tests for the constructor fairly easily, so we do that first (Note that we've included some explanation in the test file, which is always a good idea):

```
We're going to test out the constructor for the multiply
operation, first. Since all that the constructor has to do is
record all of the operands, this is straightforward.

>>> mocker = Mocker()
>>> p1 = mocker.mock()
>>> p2 = mocker.mock()
>>> mocker.replay()
>>> m = operations.multiply(p1, p2)
>>> m.operands == (p1, p2)
True
>>> mocker.restore()
>>> mocker.verify()
```

3. The tests for the `evaluate` method are somewhat more complicated, because there are several things we need to test. This is also where we start seeing the real advantages of Mocker:

```
Now we're going to check the evaluate method for the multiply
operation. It should raise a ValueError if there are less than two
operands, it should call the evaluate methods of all operations
that are operands of the multiply, and of course it should return
the correct value.

>>> mocker = Mocker()
>>> p1 = mocker.mock()
>>> p1.evaluate({}) #doctest: +ELLIPSIS
<mocker.Mock object at ...>
>>> mocker.result(97.43)

>>> mocker.replay()

>>> m = operations.multiply(p1)
>>> m.evaluate({})
Traceback (most recent call last):
ValueError: multiply without at least two operands is meaningless
>>> mocker.restore()
>>> mocker.verify()

>>> mocker = Mocker()
```

```
>>> p1 = mocker.mock()
>>> p1.evaluate({}) #doctest: +ELLIPSIS
<mocker.Mock object at ...>
>>> mocker.result(97.43)
>>> p2 = mocker.mock()
>>> p2.evaluate({}) #doctest: +ELLIPSIS
<mocker.Mock object at ...>
>>> mocker.result(-16.25)

>>> mocker.replay()

>>> m = operations.multiply(p1, p2)
>>> round(m.evaluate({}), 2)
-1583.24

>>> mocker.restore()
>>> mocker.verify()
```

4. If we run the tests now, we get a list of failed tests. Most of them are due to Mocker being unable to import the operations module, but the bottom of the list should look like this:

```
Failed example:
    mocker.verify()
Exception raised:
    Traceback (most recent call last):
      File "/usr/lib64/python2.6/doctest.py", line 1241, in __run
        compileflags, 1) in test.globs
      File "<doctest 8846_04_tfal.txt[30]>", line 1, in <module>
        mocker.verify()
      File "build/bdist.linux-x86_64/egg/mocker.py", line 503, in verify
        raise AssertionError(os.linesep.join(message))
    AssertionError: [Mocker] Unmet expectations:

    => p1.evaluate({})
     - Performed fewer times than expected.

    => p2.evaluate({})
     - Performed fewer times than expected.

**************************************************************
1 items had failures:
   9 of  31 in 8846_04_tfal.txt
***Test Failed*** 9 failures.
```

5. Finally, we'll write some code in the operations module that passes these tests, producing the following:

```
class multiply:
    def __init__(self, *operands):
        self.operands = operands

    def evaluate(self, bindings):
        vals = [x.evaluate(bindings) for x in self.operands]
```

```
        if len(vals) < 2:
            raise ValueError('multiply without at least two '
                             'operands is meaningless')
        result = 1.0
        for val in vals:
            result *= val
        return result
```

6. Now when we run the tests, none of them should fail.

What just happened?

The difficulty in writing the tests for something like this comes(as it often does) from the need to decouple the multiplication class from all of the other mathematical operation classes, so that the results of the multiplication test only depend on whether multiplication works correctly.

We addressed this problem by using the Mocker framework for mock objects. The way Mocker works is that you first create an object representing the mocking context, by doing something such as mocker = Mocker(). The mocking context will help you create mock objects, and it will store information about how you expect them to be used. Additionally, it can help you temporarily replace library objects with mocks (like we've previously done with time.time) and restore the real objects to their places when you're done. We'll see more about doing that in a little while.

Once you have a mocking context, you create a mock object by calling its mock method, and then you demonstrate how you expect the mock objects to be used. The mocking context records your demonstration, so later on when you call its replay method it knows what usage to expect for each object and how it should respond. Your tests (which use the mock objects instead of the real objects that they imitate), go after the call to replay.

Finally, after test code has been run, you call the mocking context's restore method to undo any replacements of library objects, and then verify to check that the actual usage of the mocks was as expected.

Our first use of Mocker was straightforward. We tested our constructor, which is specified to be extremely simple. It's not supposed to do anything with its parameters, aside from store them away for later. Did we gain anything at all by using Mocker to create mock objects to use as the parameters, when the parameters aren't even supposed to do anything? In fact, we did. Since we didn't tell Mocker to expect any interactions with the mock objects, it will report nearly any usage of the parameters (storing them doesn't count, because storing them isn't actually interacting with them) as errors during the verify step. When we call mocker.verify(), Mocker looks back at how the parameters were really used and reports a failure if our constructor tried to perform some action on them. It's another way to embed our expectations into our tests.

We used Mocker twice more, except in those later uses we told Mocker to expect a call to an `evaluate` method on the mock objects (i.e. `p1` and `p2`), and to expect an empty dictionary as the parameter to each of the mock objects' `evaluate` call. For each call we told it to expect, we also told it that its response should be to return a specific floating point number. Not coincidentally, that mimics the behavior of an operation object, and we can use the mocks in our tests of `multiply.evaluate`.

If `multiply.evaluate` hadn't called the `evaluate` methods of mock, or if it had called one of them more than once, our `mocker.verify` call would have alerted us to the problem. This ability to describe not just what should be called but how often each thing should be called is a very useful too that makes our descriptions of what we expect much more complete. When `multiply.evaluate` calls the `evaluate` method of mock, the values that get returned are the ones that we specified, so we know exactly what `multiply.evaluate` ought to do. We can test it thoroughly, and we can do it without involving any of the other units of our code. Try changing how `multiply.evaluate` works and see what `mocker.verify` says about it.

Mocking functions

Normal objects (that is to say, objects with methods and attributes created by instantiating a class) aren't the only things you can make mocks of. Functions are another kind of object that can be mocked, and it turns out to be pretty easy.

During your demonstration, if you want a mock object to represent a function, just call it. The mock object will recognize that you want it to behave like a function, and it will make a note of what parameters you passed it, so that it can compare them against what gets passed to it during the test.

For example, the following code creates a mock called `func`, which pretends to be a function that, when called once with the parameters `56` and `hello`, returns the number `11`. The second part of the example uses the mock in a very simple test:

```
>>> from mocker import Mocker
>>> mocker = Mocker()
>>> func = mocker.mock()
>>> func(56, "hello") # doctest: +ELLIPSIS
<mocker.Mock object at ...>
>>> mocker.result(11)

>>> mocker.replay()
>>> func(56, "hello")
11
>>> mocker.restore()
>>> mocker.verify()
```

Mocking containers

Containers are another category of somewhat special objects that can be mocked. Like functions, containers can be mocked by simply using a mock object as if it were a container during your example.

Mock objects are able to understand examples that involve the following container operations: looking up a member, setting a member, deleting a member, finding the length, and getting an iterator over the members. Depending on the version of Mocker, membership testing via the in operator may also be available.

In the following example, all of the above capabilities are demonstrated, but the in tests are disabled for compatibility with versions of Mocker that don't support them. Keep in mind that even though, after we call replay, the object called container looks like an actual container, it's not. It's just responding to stimuli we told it to expect, in the way we told it to respond. That's why, when our test asks for an iterator, it returns None instead. That's what we told it to do, and that's all it knows.

```
>>> from mocker import Mocker
>>> mocker = Mocker()
>>> container = mocker.mock()
>>> container['hi'] = 18
>>> container['hi'] # doctest: +ELLIPSIS
<mocker.Mock object at ...>
>>> mocker.result(18)
>>> len(container)
0
>>> mocker.result(1)
>>> 'hi' in container # doctest: +SKIP
True
>>> mocker.result(True)
>>> iter(container) # doctest: +ELLIPSIS
<...>
>>> mocker.result(None)
>>> del container['hi']
>>> mocker.result(None)
>>> mocker.replay()
>>> container['hi'] = 18
>>> container['hi']
18
>>> len(container)
1
```

```
>>> 'hi' in container # doctest: +SKIP
True
>>> for key in container:
...     print key
Traceback (most recent call last):
TypeError: iter() returned non-iterator of type 'NoneType'
>>> del container['hi']
>>> mocker.restore()
>>> mocker.verify()
```

Something to notice in the above example is that during the initial phase, a few of the demonstrations (for example, the call to `len`) did not return a `mocker.Mock` object, as we might have expected. For some operations, Python enforces that the result is of a particular type (for example, container lengths have to be integers), which forces Mocker to break its normal pattern. Instead of returning a generic mock object, it returns an object of the correct type, although the value of the returned object is meaningless. Fortunately, this only applies during the initial phase, when you're showing Mocker what to expect, and only in a few cases, so it's usually not a big deal. There are times when the returned mock objects are needed, though, so it's worth knowing about the exceptions.

Parameter matching

Sometimes, we would like our mocked functions and methods to accept a whole domain of parameters, instead of limiting itself to the accepting objects that compare equal to the parameters we specifically told it about. This can be useful for any number of reasons: perhaps the mock needs to accept an external variable as a parameter (the current time, or available disk space, for example), or maybe the mock example will be invoked multiple times (which we'll discuss soon), or maybe the parameters are simply not important to the definition of correct behavior.

We can tell a mock function to accept a domain of parameters by using the ANY, ARGS, KWARGS, IS, IN, CONTAINS, and MATCH special values, all of which are defined in the `mocker` module. These special values are passed to a mock object as function call parameters during its demonstration phase (before you call `replay`).

ANY

Passing ANY as a function parameter causes the object to accept any single object as its parameter in that position.

```
>>> from mocker import Mocker, ANY
>>> mocker = Mocker()
>>> func = mocker.mock()
```

```
>>> func(7, ANY) # doctest: +ELLIPSIS
<mocker.Mock object at ...>
>>> mocker.result(5)
>>> mocker.replay()
>>> func(7, 'this could be anything')
5
>>> mocker.restore()
>>> mocker.verify()
```

ARGS

Passing ARGS as a function parameter causes the object to accept any number of positional arguments, as if it had been declared with *args in its parameter list.

```
>>> from mocker import Mocker, ARGS
>>> mocker = Mocker()
>>> func = mocker.mock()
>>> func(7, ARGS) # doctest: +ELLIPSIS
<mocker.Mock object at ...>
>>> mocker.result(5)
>>> mocker.replay()
>>> func(7, 'this could be anything', 'so could this', 99.2)
5
>>> mocker.restore()
>>> mocker.verify()
```

KWARGS

Passing KWARGS as a function parameter causes the object to accept any number of keyword arguments, as if it had been declared with **kwargs in its parameter list.

```
>>> from mocker import Mocker, KWARGS
>>> mocker = Mocker()
>>> func = mocker.mock()
>>> func(7, KWARGS) # doctest: +ELLIPSIS
<mocker.Mock object at ...>
>>> mocker.result(5)
>>> mocker.replay()
>>> func(7, a='this could be anything', b='so could this')
5
>>> mocker.restore()
>>> mocker.verify()
```

IS

Passing IS(some_object) is unusual, because instead of being an inexact parameter, it's more exact than the default. Mocker will normally accept any parameter that is == to the value passed during the initial phase, but if you use IS, it instead checks whether the parameter and some_object are in fact the exact same object, and only accepts the call if they are.

```
>>> from mocker import Mocker, IS
>>> mocker = Mocker()
>>> param = [1, 2, 3]
>>> func = mocker.mock()
>>> func(7, IS(param)) # doctest: +ELLIPSIS
<mocker.Mock object at ...>
>>> mocker.result(5)
>>> mocker.replay()
>>> func(7, param) # func(7, [1, 2, 3]) would fail
5
>>> mocker.restore()
>>> mocker.verify()
```

IN

Passing IN(some_container) causes Mocker to accept any parameter that is contained in the container object called some_container.

```
>>> from mocker import Mocker, IN
>>> mocker = Mocker()
>>> func = mocker.mock()
>>> func(7, IN([45, 68, 19])) # doctest: +ELLIPSIS
<mocker.Mock object at ...>
>>> mocker.result(5)
>>> func(7, IN([45, 68, 19])) # doctest: +ELLIPSIS
<mocker.Mock object at ...>
>>> mocker.result(5)
>>> func(7, IN([45, 68, 19])) # doctest: +ELLIPSIS
<mocker.Mock object at ...>
>>> mocker.result(5)
>>> mocker.replay()
>>> func(7, 19)
5
>>> func(7, 19)
5
>>> func(7, 45)
5
>>> mocker.restore()
>>> mocker.verify()
```

CONTAINS

Passing CONTAINS(some_object) causes Mocker to accept any parameter for which some_object in parameter is True.

```
>>> from mocker import Mocker, CONTAINS
>>> mocker = Mocker()
>>> func = mocker.mock()
>>> func(7, CONTAINS(45)) # doctest: +ELLIPSIS
<mocker.Mock object at ...>
>>> mocker.result(5)
>>> mocker.replay()
>>> func(7, [12, 31, 45, 18])
5
>>> mocker.restore()
>>> mocker.verify()
```

MATCH

Finally, if none of the above lets you describe the conditions under which you want Mocker to accept a parameter as matching its expectation, you can pass MATCH(test_function). The test_function should be a function with one parameter, which will be passed the received parameter when the mocked function gets called. If the test_function returns True, the parameter is accepted.

```
>>> from mocker import Mocker, MATCH
>>> def is_odd(val):
...     return val % 2 == 1
>>> mocker = Mocker()
>>> func = mocker.mock()
>>> func(7, MATCH(is_odd)) # doctest: +ELLIPSIS
<mocker.Mock object at ...>
>>> mocker.result(5)
>>> mocker.replay()
>>> func(7, 1001)
5
>>> mocker.restore()
>>> mocker.verify()
```

Mocking complex expressions

It would be nice to be able to combine the various operations that Mocker's mock objects support. Simple attribute accesses, container member accesses and method calls make up the majority of object interactions, but they are commonly used in combinations, like `container[index].attribute.method()`. We could write a demonstration of something equivalent to this out, step-by-step, using the things we already know about Mocker's mock objects, but it would be nice to be able to just write the example as we expect it to be in the actual code.

Fortunately, we can usually do exactly that. Throughout the previous examples in this chapter, you've been seeing expressions that return `<mocker.Mock object at ...>`. Those return values are mock objects, just like the ones you create by calling `Mocker.mock`, and they can be used in the same ways. That means that as long as part of a complex expression returns a mock object during the demonstration, you can continue chaining more parts of the complex expression onto it. With something like `container[index].attribute.method()`, `container[index]` returns a mock object, attribute access on that object returns another mock object, and we call a method on that object. The method call also returns a mock object, but we don't need to do anything with it in order to correctly demonstrate our expectations.

Mocker remembers our demonstration of use, no matter how complex it is or how deeply we drill down into nested objects. Later after we call `replay`, it checks that the usage is as we described it, even for very complicated usage patterns.

Have a go hero

Try telling Mocker to expect a function call which returns a string, which is then trimmed of whitespace and split on commas, and do it all as a single complex expression.

Returning iterators

So far, we've been calling `Mocker.result` to tell Mocker that the result of evaluating a particular example expression should be some specific value. That's great for simulating most expressions, and it covers the common usage of functions and methods as well, but it doesn't really do the trick for simulating a generator, or other function that returns an iterator. To handle that, we call `Mocker.generate` instead of `Mocker.result`, like so:

```
>>> from mocker import Mocker
>>> from itertools import islice
>>> mocker = Mocker()
>>> generator = mocker.mock()
>>> generator(12) # doctest: +ELLIPSIS
<mocker.Mock object at ...>
```

```
>>> mocker.generate([16, 31, 24, 'hike'])
>>> mocker.replay()
>>> tuple(islice(generator(12), 1, 2))
(31,)
>>> mocker.restore()
>>> mocker.verify()
```

Raising exceptions

Some expressions raise an exception instead of returning a result, so we need to be able to make our mock objects do the same. Fortunately, it's not difficult: you call `Mocker.throw` to tell Mocker that the correct response to an expected expression is to raise a particular exception.

```
>>> from mocker import Mocker
>>> mocker = Mocker()
>>> obj = mocker.mock()
>>> obj.thingy # doctest: +ELLIPSIS
<mocker.Mock object at ...>
>>> mocker.throw(AttributeError('thingy does not exist'))
>>> mocker.replay()
>>> obj.thingy
Traceback (most recent call last):
AttributeError: thingy does not exist
>>> mocker.restore()
>>> mocker.verify()
```

Calling functions via a mock

Sometimes a function that we're mocking has side-effects that are important to our tests. Mocker handles these situations by allowing you to specify one or more functions that should be called, when a particular expression occurs. These functions can either be existing functions that are pulled from somewhere in your codebase, or they can be special functions that you've embedded in your test specifically to produce the desired side effects.

There is one restriction on which functions can be called as a result of interacting with one of the mock objects of Mocker: such a function must not require any parameters. This isn't as big a restriction as you might think, because you know exactly which parameters should be passed to the called functions, and so you can write a small wrapper function that just calls the target function with those parameters. This is demonstrated in the next example.

The Python `lambda` keyword is a mechanism for wrapping a single expression up as a function. When the function gets called, the expression is evaluated, and whatever the expression evaluated to is returned from the function. The uses of `lambda` are many and varied, but using it to create minor wrappers around calls to other functions is a common one.

Calling functions in this way isn't exclusive with having the mocked function return a result. In the following example, the mocked function makes two function calls and returns the number 5.

```
>>> from mocker import Mocker
>>> from sys import stdout
>>> mocker = Mocker()
>>> obj = mocker.mock()
>>> obj.method() # doctest: +ELLIPSIS
<mocker.Mock object at ...>
>>> mocker.call((lambda: stdout.write('hi')))
>>> mocker.call((lambda: stdout.write('yo\n')))
>>> mocker.result(5)
>>> mocker.replay()
>>> obj.method()
hiyo
5
>>> mocker.restore()
>>> mocker.verify()
```

Specifying that an expectation should occur multiple times

As you may have noticed in some of the preceding examples, sometimes telling Mocker what to expect can get repetitive. The example of the IN parameter matcher show this well: We did a lot of repetitive work telling Mocker that we expected three calls to the func function. That makes the test long (which reduces its readability) and it violates the DRY (Don't Repeat Yourself) principle of programming, making it harder to modify the test later on. Besides which, it's annoying to write all those duplicate expectations.

To solve this problem, Mocker allows us to specify the number of times that an expectation ought to occur during the execution of the test. We do this by calling `Mocker.count` to specify the expected number of repetitions. To see the simplest way to do that, let's re-write the `IN` example, so that we don't have to keep repeating ourselves:

```
>>> from mocker import Mocker, IN
>>> mocker = Mocker()
>>> func = mocker.mock()
>>> func(7, IN([45, 68, 19])) # doctest: +ELLIPSIS
<mocker.Mock object at ...>
>>> mocker.result(5)
>>> mocker.count(3)

>>> mocker.replay()
>>> func(7, 19)
5
>>> func(7, 19)
5
>>> func(7, 45)
5
>>> mocker.restore()
>>> mocker.verify()
```

Notice how parameter matching works well with specifying a count, letting us compress several different calls to `func` into a single expectation, even though they have different parameters. By using these two features in conjunction, the expectations of a mock can often be shortened significantly, removing redundant information. Keep in mind though, that you don't want to remove important information from a test; if it mattered that the first call to `func` had `19` as its parameter, or that the calls came in a particular order, compressing the expectation this way would lose that information, which would compromise the test.

In the above example, we specified a precise number of times to expect the call to `func` to repeat, but `count` is more flexible than that. By giving it two parameters, `count` can be told to expect any number of repetitions between a minimum and a maximum number. As long as the actual number of repetitions during the test is at least as many as the minimum number, and no more than the maximum number, Mocker will accept it as correct usage.

```
>>> from mocker import Mocker, IN
>>> mocker = Mocker()
>>> func = mocker.mock()
>>> func(7, IN([45, 68, 19])) # doctest: +ELLIPSIS
<mocker.Mock object at ...>
>>> mocker.result(5)
>>> mocker.count(1, 3)

>>> mocker.replay()
```

```
>>> func(7, 19)
5
>>> func(7, 45)
5
>>> func(7, 19)
5
>>> mocker.restore()
>>> mocker.verify()
```

Finally, it's possible to specify that an expectation is to be repeated at least a certain number of times, but with no maximum number of repetitions. As long as the expectation is met at least as many times as specified, Mocker considers its usage to have been correct. To do this, we pass None as the maximum parameter when we call count.

```
>>> from mocker import Mocker, IN
>>> mocker = Mocker()
>>> func = mocker.mock()
>>> func(7, IN([45, 68, 19])) # doctest: +ELLIPSIS
<mocker.Mock object at ...>
>>> mocker.result(5)
>>> mocker.count(1, None)
>>> mocker.replay()
>>> [func(7, 19) for x in range(50)] == [5] * 50
True
>>> mocker.restore()
>>> mocker.verify()
```

That last example uses a couple of esoteric Python features. On the left side of the == is a "list comprehension," which is a compact way of constructing a list as a transformation of another iterable. On the right is list multiplication, which creates a new list containing the members of the old list repeated a number of times—in this case, the list contains 50 repetitions of the value 5.

Replacing library objects with mocks

Several times, we've seen a need to replace something outside of our own code with a mock object: for example, time.time needed to be replaced with something that produced predictable results, in order for the tests on our PID controller to be meaningful.

Mocker provides us with a tool to address this common need, and it's quite simple to use. Mocker's mocking contexts contain a method called `replace` which behaves pretty much like `mock` from our point of view, but which is able to completely replace an existing object with a mock object, no matter what module (or modules) it exists in, or when it was imported. Even better, when we call `restore` the mock goes away, and original object is returned to its rightful place.

This gives us an easy way to isolate our tests even from library code that we couldn't normally control, and to do it without leaving any trace after we're done.

To illustrate `replace`, we're going to temporarily replace `time.time` with a mock. We've done this before—in our PID tests—in an ad hoc manner. It made our tests ugly and difficult to read. It also only replaced the name `time.time` with our mock: if we'd done `from time import time` in our PID code, the replacement wouldn't have caught it unless the replacement was done before we imported PID. Mocker will handle such complex replacements correctly, no matter when the imports occur or what form they take, with no extra effort on our part.

```
>>> from time import time
>>> from mocker import Mocker

>>> mocker = Mocker()
>>> mock_time = mocker.replace('time.time')

>>> mock_time() # doctest: +ELLIPSIS
<mocker.Mock object at ...>
>>> mocker.result(1.3)

>>> mock_time() # doctest: +ELLIPSIS
<mocker.Mock object at ...>
>>> mocker.result(2.7)

>>> mock_time() # doctest: +ELLIPSIS
<mocker.Mock object at ...>
>>> mocker.result(3.12)

>>> mocker.replay()
>>> '%1.3g' % time()
'1.3'
>>> '%1.3g' % time()
'2.7'
>>> '%1.3g' % time()
'3.12'
>>> mocker.restore()
>>> mocker.verify()
```

Notice that we imported `time` before we replace it with a mock, and yet when we actually used it, it turned out to be the mock we were using. After the call to restore, if we'd called `time` again, it would have been the real time function again.

 Why did we use string formatting on the output from `time`? We did this because floating point numbers are imprecise, meaning that the number we entered as 3.12, for example, might be represented in the system as 3.1200000000000001 or some other value that is very close to, but not precisely, 3.12. The exact value used can vary from system to system, so comparing against a float makes your tests less portable. Our string formatting rounded the number to just the relevant digits.

Pop quiz – Mocker usage

1. Which of the following would you use to check whether a parameter passed to a mock was one of a set of allowed parameters: CONTAINS, IN, IS?

2. When you specify that an expectation can repeat, how do you specify that there is no upper limit to how many times it can be repeated?

3. What does `mocker.verify()` do?

Have a go hero – mocking datetime

Take a look at the following test code, and fill in the missing Mocker demonstrations so that the test passes:

```
>>> from datetime import datetime
>>> from mocker import Mocker
>>> mocker = Mocker()
```

Here's where your Mocker demonstrations should go.

```
>>> mocker.replay()
>>> now = datetime.now()
>>> then = now.replace(hour = 12)
>>> then.isocalendar()
(2009, 24, 3)
>>> then.isoformat()
'2009-06-10T12:30:39.812555'
>>> mocker.restore()
>>> mocker.verify()
```

Mocking self

When a method of an object is called, it's first parameter is a reference to the object that contains the method. We'd like to be able to replace it with a mock, because that's the only way to truly separate each method, so that each can be tested as an individual unit. If we can't mock `self`, the methods will tend to interfere with each other's tests by interacting via their containing object.

The stumbling block in all this is that the `self` object isn't passed explicitly by the caller when a method gets called: Python already knows which object the method is bound to, and fills it in automatically. How can we substitute a mock for a parameter that doesn't come from us?

We can solve this problem by finding the function that we're testing in its class and invoking it directly, rather than invoking it as a method bound to an object. That way, we can pass all of the parameters, including the first one, without the interpreter performing any of its magic.

Time for action – passing a mock object as self

1. Remember the `testable` class that we used, among other things, to demonstrate how it can be difficult to separate methods so we can deal with them as units? Although we saw this before in Chapter 3, here it is again:

```python
class testable:
    def method1(self, number):
        number += 4
        number **= 0.5
        number *= 7
        return number

    def method2(self, number):
        return ((number * 2) ** 1.27) * 0.3

    def method3(self, number):
        return self.method1(number) + self.method2(number)

    def method4(self):
        return self.method3(id(self))
```

2. We're going to write a unit test for `method3`. Like all unit tests, it needs to not involve any code from any other unit, which in this case means that `self.method1` and `self.method2` need to be mock objects. The best way to achieve that is to have `self` itself be a mock object, so that's what we're going to do. The first step is to create a mock object that expects the interactions that `method3` ought to perform:

```
>>> from testable import testable
>>> from mocker import Mocker
>>> mocker = Mocker()

>>> target = mocker.mock()
>>> target.method1(12) # doctest: +ELLIPSIS
<mocker.Mock object at ...>
>>> mocker.result(5)
>>> target.method2(12) # doctest: +ELLIPSIS
<mocker.Mock object at ...>
>>> mocker.result(7)
```

3. `method3` is supposed to call `method1` and `method2`, and the mock we just created expects to see calls to `method1` and `method2`. So far, so good, so what's the trick to getting this mock object to be `self` for a call to `method3`? Here's the rest of the test:

```
>>> mocker.replay()
>>> testable.method3.im_func(target, 12)
12
```

What just happened?

We went to the `testable` class and looked up its `method3` member, which is something called an "unbound method object." Once we had an unbound method object, we looked inside of it for its `im_func` attribute, which is simply a function, without any of the razzmatazz associated with methods. Once we had a normal function in hand, it was easy to call it, and pass our mock object as its first parameter.

> Python version 3.0 made this easier, by getting rid of unbound method objects in favor of just storing the function object directly in the class. This means that if you're using Python 3.0 or higher, you can just call `testable.method3(target, 12)`.

Summary

We learned a lot in this chapter about mocking, and about the Python Mocker. We focused on the assorted features that Mocker provides to help you keep units separate from each other.

Specifically, we covered what mock objects are, and what they're for, how to use Python Mocker to make mocking easier, lots of ways to customize Mocker's behavior to suit your needs, and how to substitute a mock object for a method's `self` parameter.

By this time, we've started to see situations where `doctest`—simple and easy though it is—begins getting unwieldy. In the next chapter, we're going to look at Python's other built-in framework for unit testing: `unittest`.

5

When Doctest isn't Enough: Unittest to the Rescue

As the tests get more detailed (or complex), or they require more setup code to prepare the way for them, doctest begins to get a little bit annoying. The very simplicity that makes it the best way to write testable specifications and other simple tests starts to interfere with writing tests for complicated things.

In this chapter we shall:

- ◆ Learn how to write and execute tests in the unittest framework
- ◆ Learn how to express familiar testing concepts using unittest
- ◆ Discuss the specific features that make unittest suitable for more complicated testing scenarios
- ◆ Learn about of couple of Mocker's features that integrate well with unittest

So let's get on with it!

Basic unittest

Before we start talking about new concepts and features, let's take a look at how to use unittest to express the ideas that we've already learned about. That way, we'll have something solid to ground our new understanding into.

Time for action – testing PID with unittest

We'll revisit the PID class (or at least the tests for the PID class) from Chapter 3. We'll rewrite the tests so that they operate within the unittest framework.

Before moving on, take a moment to refer back to the final version of the pid.txt file from Chapter 3. We'll be implementing the same tests using the unittest framework.

1. Create a new file called test_pid.py in the same directory as pid.py. Notice that this is a .py file: unittest tests are pure python source code, rather than being plain text with source code embedded in it. That means the tests will be less useful from a documentary point of view, but grants other benefits in exchange.

2. Insert the following code into your newly-created test_pid.py (and please note that a few lines are long enough to get wrapped on the book's page):

```python
from unittest import TestCase, main
from mocker import Mocker

import pid

class test_pid_constructor(TestCase):
    def test_without_when(self):
        mocker = Mocker()
        mock_time = mocker.replace('time.time')
        mock_time()
        mocker.result(1.0)

        mocker.replay()

        controller = pid.PID(P=0.5, I=0.5, D=0.5,
                             setpoint=0, initial=12)

        mocker.restore()
        mocker.verify()

        self.assertEqual(controller.gains, (0.5, 0.5, 0.5))
        self.assertAlmostEqual(controller.setpoint[0], 0.0)
        self.assertEqual(len(controller.setpoint), 1)
        self.assertAlmostEqual(controller.previous_time, 1.0)
        self.assertAlmostEqual(controller.previous_error, -12.0)
        self.assertAlmostEqual(controller.integrated_error, 0)

    def test_with_when(self):
        controller = pid.PID(P=0.5, I=0.5, D=0.5,
                             setpoint=1, initial=12,
                             when=43)

        self.assertEqual(controller.gains, (0.5, 0.5, 0.5))
        self.assertAlmostEqual(controller.setpoint[0], 1.0)
```

```python
        self.assertEqual(len(controller.setpoint), 1)
        self.assertAlmostEqual(controller.previous_time, 43.0)
        self.assertAlmostEqual(controller.previous_error, -11.0)
        self.assertAlmostEqual(controller.integrated_error, 0)
class test_calculate_response(TestCase):
    def test_without_when(self):
        mocker = Mocker()
        mock_time = mocker.replace('time.time')
        mock_time()
        mocker.result(1.0)
        mock_time()
        mocker.result(2.0)
        mock_time()
        mocker.result(3.0)
        mock_time()
        mocker.result(4.0)
        mock_time()
        mocker.result(5.0)

        mocker.replay()

        controller = pid.PID(P=0.5, I=0.5, D=0.5,
                             setpoint=0, initial=12)

        self.assertEqual(controller.calculate_response(6), -3)
        self.assertEqual(controller.calculate_response(3), -4.5)
        self.assertEqual(controller.calculate_response(-1.5), -0.75)
        self.assertEqual(controller.calculate_response(-2.25),
-1.125)

        mocker.restore()
        mocker.verify()
    def test_with_when(self):
        controller = pid.PID(P=0.5, I=0.5, D=0.5,
                             setpoint=0, initial=12,
                             when=1)

        self.assertEqual(controller.calculate_response(6, 2), -3)
        self.assertEqual(controller.calculate_response(3, 3), -4.5)
        self.assertEqual(controller.calculate_response(-1.5, 4),
-0.75)
        self.assertEqual(controller.calculate_response(-2.25, 5),
-1.125)
if __name__ == '__main__':
    main()
```

3. Run the tests by typing:

```
$ python test_pid.py
```

```
$ python test_pid.py
....
Ran 4 tests in 0.015s

OK
```

What just happened?

Let's go through the code section and see what each part does. After that, we'll talk about what it all means when put together.

```python
from unittest import TestCase, main
from mocker import Mocker
import pid
class test_pid_constructor(TestCase):
    def test_without_when(self):
        mocker = Mocker()
        mock_time = mocker.replace('time.time')
        mock_time()
        mocker.result(1.0)
        mocker.replay()
        controller = pid.PID(P=0.5, I=0.5, D=0.5,
                             setpoint=0, initial=12)
        mocker.restore()
        mocker.verify()
        self.assertEqual(controller.gains, (0.5, 0.5, 0.5))
        self.assertAlmostEqual(controller.setpoint[0], 0.0)
        self.assertEqual(len(controller.setpoint), 1)
        self.assertAlmostEqual(controller.previous_time, 1.0)
        self.assertAlmostEqual(controller.previous_error, -12.0)
        self.assertAlmostEqual(controller.integrated_error, 0)
```

After a little bit of setup code, we have a test that the PID controller works correctly when not given a when parameter. Mocker is used to replace time.time with a mock that always returns a predictable value, and then we use several assertions to confirm that the attributes of the controller have been initialized to the expected values.

```python
    def test_with_when(self):
        controller = pid.PID(P=0.5, I=0.5, D=0.5,
                             setpoint=1, initial=12,
                             when=43)
        self.assertEqual(controller.gains, (0.5, 0.5, 0.5))
        self.assertAlmostEqual(controller.setpoint[0], 1.0)
        self.assertEqual(len(controller.setpoint), 1)
```

```
        self.assertAlmostEqual(controller.previous_time, 43.0)
        self.assertAlmostEqual(controller.previous_error, -11.0)
        self.assertAlmostEqual(controller.integrated_error, 0)
```

This test confirms that the PID constructor works correctly when the when parameter is supplied. Unlike the previous test, there's no need to use Mocker, because the outcome of the test is not supposed to be dependant on anything except the parameter values—the current time is irrelevant.

```
class test_calculate_response(TestCase):
    def test_without_when(self):
        mocker = Mocker()
        mock_time = mocker.replace('time.time')
        mock_time()
        mocker.result(1.0)
        mock_time()
        mocker.result(2.0)
        mock_time()
        mocker.result(3.0)
        mock_time()
        mocker.result(4.0)
        mock_time()
        mocker.result(5.0)
        mocker.replay()
        controller = pid.PID(P=0.5, I=0.5, D=0.5,
                             setpoint=0, initial=12)
        self.assertEqual(controller.calculate_response(6), -3)
        self.assertEqual(controller.calculate_response(3), -4.5)
        self.assertEqual(controller.calculate_response(-1.5), -0.75)
        sel+f.assertEqual(controller.calculate_response(-2.25),
-1.125)
        mocker.restore()
        mocker.verify()
```

The tests in this class describe the intended behavior of the calculate_response method. This first test checks the behavior when the optional when parameter is not supplied, and mocks time.time to make that behavior predictable.

```
    def test_with_when(self):
        controller = pid.PID(P=0.5, I=0.5, D=0.5,
                             setpoint=0, initial=12,
                             when=1)
        self.assertEqual(controller.calculate_response(6, 2), -3)
        self.assertEqual(controller.calculate_response(3, 3), -4.5)
        self.assertEqual(controller.calculate_response(-1.5, 4),
-0.75)
        self.assertEqual(controller.calculate_response(-2.25, 5),
-1.125)
```

In this test, the `when` parameter is supplied, so there is no need to mock `time.time`. We just have to check that the result is what we expected.

The actual tests that we performed are the same ones that were written in the doctest. So far, all that we see is a different way of expressing them.

The first thing to notice is that the test file is divided up into classes that inherit from `unittest.TestCase`, each of which contains one or more test methods. The name of each test method begins with the word *test*, which is how unittest recognizes that they are tests.

Each test method embodies a single test of a single unit. This gives us a convenient way to structure our tests, grouping together related tests into the same class, so that they're easier to find.

Putting each test into its own method means that each test executes in an isolated namespace, which makes it somewhat easier to keep unittest-style tests from interfering with each other, relative to doctest-style tests. It also means that unittest knows how many unit tests are in your test file, instead of simply knowing how many expressions there are (you may have noticed that doctest counts each `>>>` line as a separate test). Finally, putting each test in its own method means that each test has a name, which can be a valuable feature.

Tests in unittest don't directly care about anything that isn't part of a call to one of the assert methods of `TestCase`. That means that when we're using Mocker, we don't have to be bothered about the mock objects that get returned from demonstration expressions, unless we want to use them. It also means that we need to remember to write an assert describing every aspect of the test that we want to have checked. We'll go over the various assertion methods of `TestCase` shortly.

Tests aren't of much use, if you can't execute them. For the moment, the way we'll be doing that is by calling `unittest.main` when our test file is executed as a program by the Python interpreter. That's about the simplest way to run unittest code, but it's cumbersome when you have lots of tests spread across lots of files. We'll be learning about tools to address that problem in the next chapter.

`if __name__ == '__main__':` might look strange to you, but its meaning is fairly straight forward. When Python loads any module, it stores that module's name in a variable called `__name__` within the module (unless the module is the one passed to the interpreter on the command line). That module always gets the string `'__main__'` bound to its `__name__` variable. So, `if __name__ == '__main__':` means—if this module was executed directly from the command line.

Assertions

Assertions are the mechanism that we use to tell unittest what the important outcomes of the test are. By using appropriate assertions, we can tell unittest exactly what to expect from each test.

assertTrue

When we call `self.assertTrue(expression)`, we're telling unittest that the expression must be true in order for the test to be a success.

This is a very flexible assertion, since you can check for nearly anything by writing the appropriate boolean expression. It's also one of the last assertions you should consider using, because it doesn't tell unittest anything about the kind of comparison you're making, which means that unittest can't tell you as clearly what's gone wrong if the test fails.

For an example of this, consider the following test code which contains two tests that are guaranteed to fail:

```
from unittest import TestCase, main
class two_failing_tests(TestCase):
    def test_assertTrue(self):
        self.assertTrue(1 == 1 + 1)
    def test_assertEqual(self):
        self.assertEqual(1, 1 + 1)
if __name__ == '__main__':
    main()
```

It might seem like the two tests are interchangeable, since both test the same thing. Certainly they'll both fail (or in the unlikely event that one equals two, they'll both pass), so why prefer one over the other?

Take a look at what happens when we run the tests (and also notice that the tests were not executed in the same order as they were written; tests are totally independent of each other, so that's okay, right?):

```
$ python 8846_05_ex1.py
FF
======================================================================
FAIL: test_assertEqual (__main__.two_failing_tests)
----------------------------------------------------------------------
Traceback (most recent call last):
  File "8846_05_ex1.py", line 8, in test_assertEqual
    self.assertEqual(1, 1 + 1)
AssertionError: 1 != 2
======================================================================
FAIL: test_assertTrue (__main__.two_failing_tests)
----------------------------------------------------------------------
Traceback (most recent call last):
  File "8846_05_ex1.py", line 5, in test_assertTrue
    self.assertTrue(1 == 1 + 1)
AssertionError
----------------------------------------------------------------------
Ran 2 tests in 0.001s

FAILED (failures=2)
```

Do you see the difference? The `assertTrue` test was able to correctly determine that the test should fail, but it didn't know enough to report any useful information about why it failed. The `assertEqual` test, on the other hand, knew first of all that it was checking that two expressions were equal, and second it knew how to present the results, so that they would be most useful: by evaluating each of the expressions that it was comparing and placing a `!=` symbol between the results. It tells us both what expectation failed, and what the relevant expressions evaluate to.

assertFalse

The `assertFalse` method will succeed when the `assertTrue` method would fail, and vice versa. It has the same limits in terms of producing useful output that `assertTrue` has, and the same flexibility in terms of being able to test nearly any condition.

assertEqual

As mentioned in the `assertTrue` discussion, the `assertEqual` assertion checks that its two parameters are in fact equal, and reports a failure if they are not, along with the actual values of the parameters.

assertNotEqual

The `assertNotEqual` assertion fails whenever the `assertEqual` assertion would have succeeded, and vice versa. When it reports a failure, its output indicates that the values of the two expressions are equal, and provides you with those values.

assertAlmostEqual

As we've seen before, comparing floating point numbers can be troublesome. In particular, checking that two floating point numbers are equal is problematic, because things that you might expect to be equal—things that, mathematically, are equal—may still end up differing down among the least significant bits. Floating point numbers only compare equal when every bit is the same.

To address that problem, unittest provides `assertAlmostEqual`, which checks that two floating point values are almost the same; a small amount of difference between them is tolerated.

Lets look at this problem in action. If you take the square root of 7, and then square it, the result should be 7. Here's a pair of tests that check that fact:

```
from unittest import TestCase, main
class floating_point_problems(TestCase):
    def test_assertEqual(self):
        self.assertEqual((7.0 ** 0.5) ** 2.0, 7.0)
```

```
        def test_assertAlmostEqual(self):
            self.assertAlmostEqual((7.0 ** 0.5) ** 2.0, 7.0)
    if __name__ == '__main__':
        main()
```

The `test_assertEqual` method checks that $\boxed{7}^{-2} = 7^{\frac{1}{2}^2} = 7$, which is true in reality. In the more specialized number system available to computers, though, taking the square root of 7 and then squaring it doesn't quite get us back to 7, so this test will fail. More on that in a moment.

Test `test_assertAlmostEqual` method checks that $\boxed{7}^{-2} = 7^{\frac{1}{2}^2} \approx 7$, which even the computer will agree is true, so this test should pass.

Running those tests produces the following, although the specific number that you get back instead of 7 may vary depending on the details of the computer the tests are being run on:

```
$ python 8846_05_ex2.py
.F
======================================================================
FAIL: test_assertEqual (__main__.floating_point_problems)
----------------------------------------------------------------------
Traceback (most recent call last):
  File "8846_05_ex2.py", line 5, in test_assertEqual
    self.assertEqual((7.0 ** 0.5) ** 2.0, 7.0)
AssertionError: 7.0000000000000009 != 7.0

----------------------------------------------------------------------
Ran 2 tests in 0.001s

FAILED (failures=1)
```

Unfortunately, floating point numbers are not precise, because the majority of numbers on the real number line can not be represented with a finite, non-repeating sequence of digits, much less a mere 64 bits. Consequently, what you get back from evaluating the mathematical expression is not quite 7. It's close enough for government work though—or practically any other sort of work as well—so we don't want our test to quibble over that tiny difference. Because of that, we should use `assertAlmostEqual` and `assertNotAlmostEqual` when we're comparing floating point numbers for equality.

 This problem doesn't generally carry over into other comparison operators. Checking that one floating point number is less than the other, for example, is very unlikely to produce the wrong result due to insignificant errors. It's only in cases of equality that this problem bites us.

assertNotAlmostEqual

The `assertNotAlmostEqual` assertion fails whenever the `assertAlmostEqual` assertion would have succeeded, and vice versa. When it reports a failure, its output indicates that the values of the two expressions are nearly equal, and provides you with those values.

assertRaises

As always, we need to make sure that our units correctly signal errors. Doing the right thing when they receive good inputs is only half the job; they need to do something reasonable when they receive bad inputs, as well.

The `assertRaises` method checks that a callable (a callable is a function, a method, or a class. A callable can also be an object of any arbitrary type, so long as it has a __call__ method) raises a specified exception, when passed a specified set of parameters.

This assertion only works with callables, which means that you don't have a way of checking that other sorts of expressions raise an expected exception. If that doesn't fit the needs of your test, it's possible to construct your own test using the `fail` method, described below.

To use `assertRaises`, first pass it the expected exception, then pass the callable, and then the parameters that should be passed to the callable when it's invoked.

Here's an example test using `assertRaises`. This test ought to fail, because the callable won't raise the expected exception. `'8ca2'` is perfectly acceptable input to `int`, when you're also passing it `base = 16`. Notice that `assertRaises` will accept any number of positional or keyword arguments, and pass them on to the callable on invocation.

```
from unittest import TestCase, main

class silly_int_test(TestCase):
    def test_int_from_string(self):
        self.assertRaises(ValueError, int, '8ca2', base = 16)

if __name__ == '__main__':
    main()
```

When we run that test, it fails (as we knew it would) because `int` didn't raise the exception we told `assertRaises` to expect.

```
$ python 8846_05_ex3.py
F
================================================================
FAIL: test_int_from_string (__main__.silly_int_test)
----------------------------------------------------------------
Traceback (most recent call last):
  File "8846_05_ex3.py", line 5, in test_int_from_string
    self.assertRaises(ValueError, int, '8ca2', base = 16)
AssertionError: ValueError not raised

----------------------------------------------------------------
Ran 1 test in 0.001s

FAILED (failures=1)
```

If an exception is raised, but it's not the one you told unittest to expect, unittest considers that an error. An error is different from a failure. A failure means that one of your tests has detected a problem in the unit it's testing. An error means that there's a problem with the test itself.

fail

When all else fails, you can fall back on `fail`. When the code in your test calls `fail`, the test fails.

What good does that do? When none of the assert methods does what you need, you can instead write your checks in such a way that `fail` will be called if the test does not pass. This allows you to use the full expressiveness of Python to describe checks for your expectations.

Let's take a look at an example. This time, we're going to test on a less-than operation, which isn't one of the operations directly supported by an assert method. Using `fail`, it's easy to implement the test anyhow.

```python
from unittest import TestCase, main

class test_with_fail(TestCase):
    def test_less_than(self):
        if not (2.3 < 5.6):
            self.fail('2.3 is not less than 5.6, but it should be')

if __name__ == '__main__':
    main()
```

A couple of things to notice here: first of all, take note of the `not` in the `if` statement. Since we want to run `fail` if the test should not pass, but we're used to describing the circumstances when the test should succeed, a good way to write the test is to write the success condition, and then invert it with `not`. That way we can continue thinking in the way we're used to when we use fail. The second thing to note is that you can pass a message to fail when you call it, which will be printed out in unittest's report of failed tests. If you choose your message carefully, it can be a big help.

There's no screen capture of what to expect from running this test, because the test should pass, and the report wouldn't contain anything interesting. You might experiment with changing the test around and running it, to see what happens.

Pop quiz – basic unittest knowledge

1. What is the unittest equivalent of this doctest?

```
>>> try:
...     int('123')
... except ValueError:
...     pass
... else:
...     print 'Expected exception was not raised'
```

2. How do you check whether two floating point numbers are equal?

3. When would you choose to use `assertTrue`? How about `fail`?

Have a go hero – translating into unittest

Look back at some of the tests we write in the previous chapters, and translate them from doctests into unittests. Given what you already know of unittest, you should be able to translate any of the tests.

While you're doing this, think about the relative merits of unittest and doctest for each of the tests you translate. The two systems have different strengths, so it makes sense that each will be the more appropriate choice for different situations. When is doctest the better choice, and when is unittest?

Test fixtures

Unittest has an important and highly useful capability that doctest lacks. You can tell unittest how to create a standardized environment for your unit tests to run inside, and how to clean up that environment when it's done. This ability to create and destroy a standardized test environment is a test fixture. While test fixtures doesn't actually make any tests possible that were impossible before, they can certainly make them shorter and less repetitive.

Time for action – testing database-backed units

Many programs need to access a database for their operation, which means that many of the units those programs are made of also access a database. The point is that the purpose of a database is to store information and make it accessible in arbitrary other places (in other words, databases exist to break the isolation of units). (The same problem applies to other information stores as well: for example, files in permanent storage.)

How do we deal with that? After all, just leaving the units that interact with the database untested is no solution. We need to create an environment where the database connection works as usual, but where any changes that are made do not last. There are a few different ways we could do that, but no matter what the details are, we need to set up the special database connection before each test that uses it, and we need to destroy any changes after each such test.

Unittest helps us to do that by providing test fixtures via the setUp and tearDown methods of the TestCase class. These methods exist for us to override, with the default versions doing nothing.

Here's some database-using code (let's say it exists in a file called employees.py), for which we'll write tests:

This code uses the sqlite3 database which ships with Python. Since the sqlite3 interface is compatible with Python's DB-API 2.0, any database backend that you find yourself using will have a similar interface to what you see here.

```
class employees:
    def __init__(self, connection):
        self.connection = connection
    def add_employee(self, first, last, date_of_employment):
        cursor = self.connection.cursor()
        cursor.execute('''insert into employees
                            (first, last, date_of_employment)
                        values
                            (:first, :last, :date_of_
employment)''',
                        locals())
        self.connection.commit()
        return cursor.lastrowid
    def find_employees_by_name(self, first, last):
        cursor = self.connection.cursor()
        cursor.execute('''select * from employees
                        where
                            first like :first
```

```
                    and
                        last like :last''',
                    locals())
        for row in cursor:
            yield row
    def find_employees_by_date(self, date):
        cursor = self.connection.cursor()
        cursor.execute('''select * from employees
                        where date_of_employment = :date''',
                    locals())
        for row in cursor:
            yield row
```

1. We'll start writing the tests by importing the modules that we need and introducing our `TestCase` class.

```
from unittest import TestCase, main
from sqlite3 import connect, PARSE_DECLTYPES
from datetime import date
from employees import employees

class test_employees(TestCase):
```

2. We need a `setUp` method to create the environment that our tests depend on. In this case, that means creating a new database connection to an in-memory-only database, and populating that database with the needed tables and rows.

```
    def setUp(self):
        connection = connect(':memory:',
                            detect_types=PARSE_DECLTYPES)
        cursor = connection.cursor()
        cursor.execute('''create table employees
                        (first text,
                         last text,
                         date_of_employment date)''')
        cursor.execute('''insert into employees
                        (first, last, date_of_employment)
                        values
                        ("Test1", "Employee", :date)''',
                    {'date': date(year = 2003,
                                  month = 7,
                                  day = 12)})
        cursor.execute('''insert into employees
                        (first, last, date_of_employment)
                        values
                        ("Test2", "Employee", :date)''',
                    {'date': date(year = 2001,
                                  month = 3,
                                  day = 18)})

        self.connection = connection
```

3. We need a `tearDown` method to undo whatever the `setUp` method did, so that each test can run in an untouched version of the environment. Since the database is only in memory, all we have to do is close the connection, and it goes away. `tearDown` may end up being much more complicated in other scenarios.

```python
def tearDown(self):
    self.connection.close()
```

4. Finally, we need the tests themselves, and the code to execute the tests.

```python
def test_add_employee(self):
    to_test = employees(self.connection)
    to_test.add_employee('Test1', 'Employee', date.today())
    cursor = self.connection.cursor()
    cursor.execute('''select * from employees
                      order by date_of_employment''')
    self.assertEqual(tuple(cursor),
                        (('Test2', 'Employee', date(year=2001,
                                                    month=3,
                                                    day=18)),
                            ('Test1', 'Employee', date(year=2003,
                                                       month=7,
                                                       day=12)),
                            ('Test1', 'Employee', date.today())))
def test_find_employees_by_name(self):
    to_test = employees(self.connection)
    found = tuple(to_test.find_employees_by_name('Test1',
'Employee'))
    expected = (('Test1', 'Employee', date(year=2003,
                                            month=7,
                                            day=12)),)
    self.assertEqual(found, expected)
def test_find_employee_by_date(self):
    to_test = employees(self.connection)
    target = date(year=2001, month=3, day=18)
    found = tuple(to_test.find_employees_by_date(target))
    expected = (('Test2', 'Employee', target),)
    self.assertEqual(found, expected)
if __name__ == '__main__':
    main()
```

What just happened?

We used a `setUp` method for our `TestCase`, along with a matching `tearDown` method. Between them, these methods made sure that the environment in which the tests were executed was the one they needed (that was `setUp`'s job) and that the environment of each test was cleaned up after the test was run, so that the tests didn't interfere with each other (which was the job of `tearDown`). Unittest made sure that `setUp` was run once before each test method, and that `tearDown` was run once after each test method.

Because a test fixture—as defined by `setUp` and `tearDown`—gets wrapped around every test in a `TestCase` class, the `setUp` and `tearDown` for `TestCase` classes that contain too many tests can get very complicated and waste a lot of time dealing with details that are unnecessary for some of the tests. You can avoid that problem by simply grouping together, those tests that require specific aspects of the environment into their own `TestCase` classes. Give each `TestCase` an appropriate `setUp` and `tearDown`, only dealing with those aspects of the environment that are necessary for the tests it contains. You can have as many `TestCase` classes as you want, so there's no need to skimp on them when you're deciding which tests to group together.

Notice how simple the `tearDown` method that we used was. That's usually a good sign: when the changes that need to be undone in the `tearDown` method are simple to describe, it often means that you can be sure of doing it perfectly. Since any imperfection of the `tearDown` makes it possible for tests to leave behind stray data that might alter how other tests behave, getting it right is important. In this case, all of our changes were confined to the database, so getting rid of the database does the trick.

Pop quiz – test fixtures

1. What is the purpose of a test fixture?
2. How is a test fixture created?.
3. Can a test fixture have a `tearDown` method without a `setUp`? How about `setUp` without `tearDown`?

Have a go hero – file path abstraction

Below is a class definition that describes an abstraction of file paths. Your challenge is to write unit tests (using unittest) that check each of the methods of the class, making sure that they behave as advertised. You will need to use a test fixture to create and destroy a sandbox area in the filesystem for your tests to operate on.

Because doctest doesn't support test fixtures, writing these tests using that framework would be quite annoying. You'd have to duplicate the code to create the environment before each test, and the code to clean it up after each test. By using `unittest`, we can avoid that duplication.

There are several things about this class that are wrong, or at least not as right as they ought to be. See if you can catch them with your tests.

```python
from os.path import isfile, isdir, exists, join
from os import makedirs, rmdir, unlink
class path:
    r"""

    Instances of this class represent a file path, and facilitate
    several operations on files and directories.

    Its most surprising feature is that it overloads the division
    operator, so that the result of placing a / operator between two
    paths (or between a path and a string) results in a longer path,
    representing the two operands joined by the system's path
    separator character.
    """
    def __init__(self, target):
        self.target = target
    def exists(self):
        return exists(self.target)
    def isfile(self):
        return isfile(self.target)
    def isdir(self):
        return isdir(self.target)
    def mkdir(self, mode = 493):
        makedirs(self.target, mode)
    def rmdir(self):
        if self.isdir():
            rmdir(self.target)
        else:
            raise ValueError('Path does not represent a directory')
    def delete(self):
        if self.exists():
            unlink(self.target)
        else:
            raise ValueError('Path does not represent a file')
    def open(self, mode = "r"):
        return open(self.target, mode)
    def __div__(self, other):
        if isinstance(other, path):
            return path(join(self.target, other.target))
        return path(join(self.target, other))

    def __repr__(self):
        return '<path %s>' % self.target
```

Integrating with Python Mocker

You've used Mocker enough to see the repetitiveness involved in creating a mocking context at the beginning of the text and calling its `verify` and `restore` methods at the end. Mocker simplifies this for you by providing a class called `MockerTestCase` in the mocker module. `MockerTestCase` behaves just like a normal unittest `TestCase`, except that for each test, it automatically creates a mocking context, which it then verifies and restores after the test. The mocking context is stored in `self.mocker`.

The following example demonstrates `MockerTestCase` by using it to write a test involving a mock of `time.time`. Before the test gets executed, a mocking context is stored in `self.mocker`. After the test is run, the context is automatically verified and restored.

```
from unittest import main
from mocker import MockerTestCase
from time import time
class test_mocker_integration(MockerTestCase):
    def test_mocking_context(self):
        mocker = self.mocker
        time_mock = mocker.replace('time.time')
        time_mock()
        mocker.result(1.0)
        mocker.replay()
        self.assertAlmostEqual(time(), 1.0)
if __name__ == '__main__':
    main()
```

The above is a simple test that checks that the current time is `1.0`, which it would not be if we didn't mock `time.time`. Instead of creating a new Mocker instance, we have one already available to us as `self.mocker`, so we use that. We also get to leave off the calls to `verify` and `restore`, because the `MockerTestCase` takes care of that for us.

Summary

This chapter contained a lot of information about how to use the unittest framework to write your tests.

Specifically, we covered how to use unittest to express concepts that you were already familiar with from doctest, differences and similarities between unittest and doctest, how to use test fixtures to embed your tests in a controlled and temporary environment, and how to use Python Mocker's `MockerTestCase` to simplify the integration of unittest and Mocker.

Until now, we've been running tests individually, or in small groups, by directly instructing Python to run them. Now that we've learned about unittest, we're ready to talk about managing and executing large bodies of tests, which is the topic of the next chapter.

6

Running Your Tests: Follow Your Nose

So far, we've talked a lot about how to write tests, but we haven't said much about how to run them. We've had to explicitly tell Python which tests to run, and we've had the either worry about which version of Python we were using (in the case of doctest) or put an `if __name__ == '__main__'` *inside every module (for unittest). Clearly, there's room for improvement, when it comes to running tests.*

In this chapter we shall:

◆ Learn about a Python tool called Nose, which automatically finds and executes tests

◆ Learn how to make Nose find and execute doctest tests

◆ Learn how to make Nose find and execute unittest tests

◆ Learn how to use Nose's internal test framework

So let's get on with it!

What is Nose?

Nose is a tool for finding and running all of your tests, in one easy step. It finds tests in multiple files, organizes them, runs them, and presents you with a nice report at the end. You don't have to put any special code in your files to make the tests runnable and you don't have to worry about which Python version you're running, unless your tests make use of recently added features to the language. Nose understands doctest and unittest tests; it even adds a few features to both.

Installing Nose

At the time of this writing, Nose's home page is `http://code.google.com/p/python-nose/`, with downloads available at `http://code.google.com/p/python-nose/downloads/list`. Go ahead and download the latest version, and uncompress it into a temporary directory. If you're using Windows, you'll need a program such as 7-Zip (`http://7-zip.org/`) to uncompress the file; Linux and Mac users won't need any special software.

After uncompressing Nose, we need to install it. Everything we had to consider when installing Mocker applies here too: If you installed Python, you can just change to the Nose directory and type:

```
$ python setup.py install
```

If you didn't install Python, but you're using version 2.6 or higher, you can instead type:

```
$ python setup.py install --user
```

If you go for the `--user` installation, you might need to add a directory to the search path of your operating system. You'll know you need to if you can't run the `nosetests` program after installing it. On Linux or Mac, the directory that you need to add is `~/.local/bin`, while on Windows it's `%APPDATA%\Python\Scripts`. Additionally, on Windows you may need to create a file called `nosetests.bat` in the `%APPDATA%\Python\Scripts` directory, containing the line: `@python %APPDATA%\Python\Scripts\nosetests`.

Sometimes, a tool called `easy_install` can simplify the installation process of Python modules and packages. If you want to give it a try, download and install setuptools from `http://pypi.python.org/pypi/setuptools`, and then run the command easy_install nose. Once that command is executed, you should be ready to use Nose.

After installing it, you should be able to run `nosetests` by typing its name on the command line. If you run it in an empty directory, you should see output similar to this:

```
$ nosetests
----------------------------------------------------------------------
Ran 0 tests in 0.007s

OK
```

Organizing tests

All right, we've got Nose installed, so what's it good for? Nose looks through a directory's structure, finds the test files, sorts out the tests that they contain, runs the tests, and reports the results back to you. That's a lot of work that it saves you from having to do each time you want to run your tests (which should be often).

Nose recognizes test files based on their names. Any file whose name contains `test` or `Test` either at the beginning or following any of the characters _, ., or – (this is often referred to as "underscore", dot, or dash) is recognized as a file that contains unittest `TestCases` (or Nose's own test functions, which we'll talk about later) which should be executed. Any directory whose name matches the same pattern is recognized as a directory that might contain tests, and so should be searched for test files. Nose can find and execute doctest tests as well, either embedded in docstrings or written in separate test files. By default, it won't look for doctest tests unless we tell it to. We'll see how to change the default shortly.

Since Nose is so willing to go looking for our tests, we have a lot of freedom with respect to how we organize them. It often turns out to be a good idea to separate all of the tests into their own directory, or for larger projects into a whole tree of directories. A big project can end up having thousands of tests, so organizing them for easy navigation is a big benefit. If doctests are being used as documentation, as well as testing, it's probably a good idea to store them in yet another separate directory, with a name that communicates that they are documentary. For a moderately-sized project, the recommended structure might look like the following:

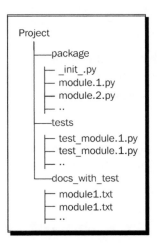

```
Project
    ├──package
    │   ├── _init_.py
    │   ├── module.1.py
    │   ├── module.2.py
    │   ├── ..
    ├──tests
    │   ├── test_module.1.py
    │   ├── test_module.1.py
    │   ├── ..
    └──docs_with_test
        ├── module1.txt
        ├── module1.txt
        ├── ..
```

That structure is only a recommendation (it's for your benefit, not for Nose's). If a different structure would make things easier for you, go ahead and use it.

Time for action – organizing tests from previous chapters

We're going to take our tests from the previous chapters and organize them all into a tree of directories. Then we'll use Nose to run them all.

1. Create a directory to hold our code and tests; you can choose any name for it, but I'll refer to it as `project` here.

2. Put `pid.py`, `operations.py` and `testable.py` inside of `project`. When we run `nosetests` in the `project` directory, modules (and packages) stored in `project` will be accessible to all of the tests, no matter where the test is stored in the directory tree.

3. Create a subdirectory called `test_chapter2`, and place the `test.txt` and `test.py` files from Chapter 2 in it.

4. Create a subdirectory called `test_chapter3`, and place the final `pid.txt` file from Chapter 3 in it.

5. Create a subdirectory called `test_chapter4`, and place the code from the Chapter 4 examples (if you have them) and *Time for action* sections in it.

6. Create a subdirectory called `test_chapter5`, and place the code from the Chapter 5 examples (if you have them) and *Time for action* sections into it. Because Chapter 5 uses unittest tests, we also need to rename each of the files so that Nose will recognize them as test files. Good names for the files are:

    `test_equal_and_almost_equal.py`, `test_fail.py`, `test_mocker_test_case.py`, `test_pid.py`, `test_raises.py`, `test_setup_teardown.py`, `test_true_and_false.py`.

7. Now that you have the tests all put together and organized, let's run them. To do that, change to the `project` directory and type:

    ```
    $ nosetests --with-doctest --doctest-extension=txt -v
    ```

 You can leave off the `-v` if you want. All it does is to tell Nose to give a more detailed report of what it's doing.

8. All of the tests should run. We expect to see a few failures, since some of the tests from previous chapters were intended to fail, for illustrative purposes. There's one failure though, that we need to consider:

```
FAIL: Doctest: pid.txt
--------------------------------------------------------------------
Traceback (most recent call last):
  File "/usr/lib64/python2.6/doctest.py", line 2131, in runTest
    raise self.failureException(self.format_failure(new.getvalue()))
AssertionError: Failed doctest test for pid.txt
  File "/home/djarb/writing/book/tests/test_chapter3/pid.txt", line 0

--------------------------------------------------------------------
File "/home/djarb/writing/book/tests/test_chapter3/pid.txt", line 16, in pid.txt
Failed example:
    controller.previous_time
Expected:
    1.0
Got:
    1246735044.6053569
--------------------------------------------------------------------
====================================================================
```

9. The first part of that error report can be safely ignored: it just means that the whole doctest file is being treated as a failing test by Nose. The useful information comes in the second part of the report. It's telling us that where we expected to get a previous time of 1.0, we're instead getting a very large number (which will be different, and larger, when you run the test for yourself, since it happens to represent the time in seconds since a point several decades in the past). What's going on? Didn't we replace `time.time` for that test with a mock? Let's take a look at the relevant part of `pid.txt`:

```
>>> import time
>>> real_time = time.time
>>> time.time = (float(x) for x in xrange(1, 1000)).next
>>> import pid
>>> controller = pid.PID(P = 0.5, I = 0.5, D = 0.5, setpoint = 0,
...                      initial = 12)
>>> controller.gains
(0.5, 0.5, 0.5)
>>> controller.setpoint
[0.0]
>>> controller.previous_time
1.0
```

10. We mocked `time.time`, but we did it the ad hoc way instead of by using Mocker's `replace` method. This means that modules which did a `from time import time` and were imported before the test file is executed will have imported the real `time` function, and won't know about our mock. So, was `pid.py` imported by some other thing, before `pid.txt` imported it? As it happens, it was: Nose itself imported it when it was scanning for tests to execute. If we're using Nose, we can't count on our import statements actually being the first to import any given module. We can fix the problem easily, though, by using Mocker (Note that we're only looking at the first test in the file here. There is another test that also needs to be fixed in the same way):

```
>>> from mocker import Mocker
>>> mocker = Mocker()
>>> mock_time = mocker.replace('time.time')
>>> t = mock_time()
>>> mocker.result(1.0)
>>> mocker.replay()
>>> import pid
>>> controller = pid.PID(P = 0.5, I = 0.5, D = 0.5, setpoint = 0,
...                      initial = 12)
>>> controller.gains
(0.5, 0.5, 0.5)
>>> controller.setpoint
[0.0]
>>> controller.previous_time
1.0
>>> controller.previous_error
-12.0
>>> controller.integrated_error
0.0
>>> mocker.restore()
>>> mocker.verify()
```

11. Now when we use nosetests to run the tests again, the only failures are the expected ones. Here's the overview that Nose prints because we passed the -v command line option:

```
$ nosetests --with-doctest --doctest-extension=txt -v
Doctest: testable ... ok
Doctest: test.txt ... FAIL
Doctest: pid.txt ... ok
Doctest: example1.txt ... ok
Doctest: example10.txt ... ok
Doctest: example11.txt ... ok
Doctest: example12.txt ... ok
Doctest: example13.txt ... ok
Doctest: example14.txt ... ok
Doctest: example15.txt ... ok
Doctest: example16.txt ... ok
Doctest: example2.txt ... ok
Doctest: example3.txt ... ok
Doctest: example4.txt ... ok
Doctest: example5.txt ... ok
Doctest: example6.txt ... ok
Doctest: example7.txt ... ok
Doctest: example8.txt ... ok
Doctest: example9.txt ... ok
Doctest: tfa1.txt ... ok
Doctest: tfa2.txt ... ok
test_assertAlmostEqual (test_equal_and_almost_equal.floating_point_problems) ... ok
test_assertEqual (test_equal_and_almost_equal.floating_point_problems) ... FAIL
test_less_than (test_fail.test_with_fail) ... ok
test_mocking_context (test_mocker_test_case.test_mocker_integration) ... ok
test_with_when (test_pid.test_calculate_response) ... ok
test_without_when (test_pid.test_calculate_response) ... ok
test_with_when (test_pid.test_pid_constructor) ... ok
test_without_when (test_pid.test_pid_constructor) ... ok
test_int_from_string (test_raises.silly_int_test) ... FAIL
test_add_employee (test_setup_teardown.test_employees) ... ok
test_find_employee_by_date (test_setup_teardown.test_employees) ... ok
test_find_employees_by_name (test_setup_teardown.test_employees) ... ok
test_assertEqual (test_true_and_false.two_failing_tests) ... FAIL
test_assertTrue (test_true_and_false.two_failing_tests) ... FAIL
```

What just happened?

We ran all of those tests, with a single command. Pretty good, right? We're getting to the point now where testing is becoming broadly useful.

Thanks to Nose, we don't need those goofy if __name__ == '__main__' blocks at the end of each unittest file, and we don't need to memorize any arcane commands to execute the doctest files. We can store our tests in a separate and well-organized directory structure, and run them all with a single, quick, and simple command. We can also easily run a subset of our tests, by passing the filenames, module names, or directories containing the tests that we want to run as command line parameters.

We also saw how hidden assumptions can break tests, just as they can break the code being tested. Until now, we've been assuming that when one of our tests imports a module, that's the first time the module has been imported. Some of our tests relied on that assumption to replace library objects with mocks. Now that we're dealing with running many tests aggregated together, with no guaranteed order of execution, that assumption wasn't reliable. On top of that, the module we had trouble with actually had to be imported to search it for tests, before any of our tests were run. That would have been a problem, except we already have a tool for replacing library objects, regardless of the order of imports. A quick switch of the affected tests to use Mocker and we're good to go.

Finding doctests

The `nosetests` command that we used in the previous section was fairly easy to understand, but it was still a bit long to type in all of the time. Instead of:

```
$ nosetests --with-doctest --doctest-extension=txt -v
```

We'd really like to be able to just type:

```
$ nosetests -v
```

Or even:

```
$ nosetests
```

To execute our tests, and still have it find and execute all of our doctests.

Fortunately, it's a simple matter to tell Nose that we want it to use different defaults for the values of those command line switches. To do this, just create a configuration file called `nose.cfg` or `.noserc` (either name will work) in your home directory, and placing the following inside of it:

```
[nosetests]
with-doctest=1
doctest-extension=txt
```

From now on, whenever you run `nosetests`, it will assume those options, unless you tell it otherwise. You don't have to type them on the command line any more. You can use the same trick for any option that Nose can accept on the command line.

If you're a Windows user, you might not be sure what the phrase 'home directory' is supposed to refer to in this context. As far as Python is concerned, your home directory is defined by your environment variables. If HOME is defined, that's your home directory. Otherwise, if USERPROFILE is defined (it usually is, pointing at `C:\Documents and Settings\USERNAME`) then that's what is considered to be your home directory. Otherwise, the directory described by HOMEDRIVE and HOMEPATH (often `C:\`)is your home directory.

Customizing Nose's search

We've said before that Nose looks for tests in directories and modules whose names start with test or Test, or contain a ' _ ', ' . ', or ' - ' followed by test or Test. That's the default, but it's not actually the whole story.

If you know regular expressions, you can customize the pattern that Nose uses to look for tests. You do this by passing the --include=REGEX command line option or by putting include=REGEX in your nose.cfg or .noserc.

For example, if you do this:

```
nosetests --include="(?:^[Dd]oc)"
```

Nose will (in addition to looking for names as described above) also look for names that start with doc or Doc. That means you can call the directory containing your doctest files docs, Documentation, doctests, and so on, and Nose will still find it and run the tests. If you use this option often, you'll almost certainly want to add it to your configuration file, as described under the previous heading.

> The full syntax and use of regular expressions is a subject in itself, and has been the topic of many books. However, you can find everything you need, to do this sort of thing in the Python documentation at http://docs.python.org/library/re.html.

Pop quiz – testing with Nose

1. By running nosetests --processes=4, Nose can be made to launch four testing processes, which can provide a big performance gain if you're running the tests on a quad-core system. How would you make Nose always launch four testing processes, without being told on the command line?

2. If some of your tests were stored in a directory called specs, how would you tell Nose that it should search that directory for tests?

3. Which of the following will by default be recognized by Nose as possibly containing tests: UnitTests, unit_tests, TestFiles, test_files, doctests?

Have a go hero – nosing around

Write some `doctest` and `unittest` tests for the following specification, and create a directory tree to contain them and the code that they describe. Write the code using the test-driven methodology, and use Nose to run the tests.

> The graph module contains two classes: Node and Arc. An Arc is a connection between two Nodes. Each Node is an intersection of an arbitrary number of Arcs.
>
> Arc objects contain references to the Node objects that the Arc connects, a textual identification label, and a "cost" or "weight", which is a real number.
>
> Node objects contain references to all of the connected Arcs, and a textual identification label.
>
> Node objects have a find_cycle(self, length) method which returns a list of Arcs making up the lowest cost complete path from the Node back to itself, if such a path exists with a length greater than 2 Arcs and less than or equal to the length parameter.
>
> Node and Arc objects have a __repr__(self) method which returns a representation involving the identification labels assigned to the objects.

Nose and doctest

Nose doesn't just support doctest, it actually enhances it. When you're using Nose, you can write test fixtures for your doctest files.

If you pass `--doctest-fixtures=_fixture` on the command line, Nose will go looking for a fixture file whenever it finds a doctest file. The name of the fixture file is based on the name of the doctest file and is calculated by appending the doctest fixture suffix (in other words, the value of `doctest-fixtures`) to the main part of the doctest file name, and then adding `.py` to the end. For example, if Nose found a doctest file called `pid.txt`, and had been told that `doctest-fixtures=_fixture`, it would try to find the test fixture in a file called `pid_fixture.py`.

The test fixture file for a doctest is very simple: it's just a Python module that contains a `setup()` or `setUp()` function and a `teardown()` or `tearDown()` function. The setup function is executed before the doctest file, and the teardown function is executed after.

The fixture operates in a different namespace to the doctest file, so none of the variables that get defined in the fixture module are visible in the actual tests. If you want to share variables between the fixture and the test, you'll probably want to do it by making a simple little module to hold the variables, which you can import into both the fixture and the test.

Mocker replacements work fine when done in a doctest fixture. As long as you don't `restore()` them during the setup (and why would you do a silly thing like that?) then they'll still be in place when the test uses the replaced object.

Time for action – creating a fixture for a doctest

We'll provide a mock `time.time()` in our test fixture and use it in our doctest.

1. Create a file called `times.txt` containing the following doctest code:

    ```
    >>> from time import time
    ```

    This isn't a reasonable test for any purpose, but it serves to illustrate a test that can't work without a mock object in place.

    ```
    >>> '%0.1f' % time()
    '1.0'
    >>> '%0.1f' % time()
    '1.1'
    >>> '%0.1f' % time()
    '1.2'
    ```

2. Run the doctest file using Nose, and the following screen gets displayed:

```
$ nosetests
F
==========================================================================
FAIL: Doctest: times.txt
--------------------------------------------------------------------------
Traceback (most recent call last):
  File "/usr/lib64/python2.6/doctest.py", line 2131, in runTest
    raise self.failureException(self.format_failure(new.getvalue()))
AssertionError: Failed doctest test for times.txt
  File "/home/djarb/writing/book/tests/test_chapter6/times.txt", line 0

--------------------------------------------------------------------------
File "/home/djarb/writing/book/tests/test_chapter6/times.txt", line 6, in times.txt
Failed example:
    '%0.1f' % time()
Expected:
    '1.0'
Got:
    '1247857750.6'
--------------------------------------------------------------------------
File "/home/djarb/writing/book/tests/test_chapter6/times.txt", line 8, in times.txt
Failed example:
    '%0.1f' % time()
Expected:
    '1.1'
Got:
    '1247857750.6'
--------------------------------------------------------------------------
File "/home/djarb/writing/book/tests/test_chapter6/times.txt", line 10, in times.txt
Failed example:
    '%0.1f' % time()
Expected:
    '1.2'
Got:
    '1247857750.6'


--------------------------------------------------------------------------
Ran 1 test in 0.021s
```

3. Unless your computer's clock was reset to the beginning of the epoch at just the right moment, the doctest failed. We need a mock to replace `time.time()` if we want these tests to pass reliably. Create a file called `times_fixture.py` and insert the following Python code:

```python
from mocker import Mocker

mocker = Mocker()

def setup():
    fake_time = mocker.replace('time.time')

    fake_time()
    mocker.result(1.0)
    fake_time()
    mocker.result(1.1)
    fake_time()
    mocker.result(1.2)

    mocker.replay()

def teardown():
    mocker.restore()
    mocker.verify()
```

4. Now when we run Nose and tell it how to find doctest fixtures, the doctest passes, because it's using the mock that we set up in the fixture:

```
$ nosetests --doctest-fixtures=_fixture
.
--------------------------------------------------------------
Ran 1 test in 0.028s

OK
$
```

5. If you use this facility often, it makes sense to add `doctest-fixtures=_fixture` to your Nose configuration file.

Nose and unittest

Nose enhances unittest, by providing test fixtures at the package and module levels. The package setup function is run before any of the tests in any of the modules in a package, while the teardown function is run after all of the tests in all of the modules in the package have completed. Similarly, the module setup is run before any of the tests in a given module execute, and the module teardown is executed after all of the tests in the module have been executed.

Time for action – creating a module fixture

We'll build a test module with a module-level fixture. In the fixture, we'll replace the `datetime.date.today` function, which normally returns an object representing the current date. We want it to return a specific value, so that our tests can know what to expect.

1. Create a directory called `tests`. We'll use this directory in this *Time for action*, as well as in the next one.

2. Within the `tests` directory, create a file called `module_fixture_tests.py` containing the following code:

```python
from unittest import TestCase
from mocker import Mocker
from datetime import date

mocker = Mocker()

def setup():
    fake_date = mocker.replace(date)

    fake_date.today()
    mocker.result(date(year = 2009, month = 6, day = 12))
    mocker.count(1, None)

    mocker.replay()

def teardown():
    mocker.restore()
    mocker.verify()

class first_tests(TestCase):
    def test_year(self):
        self.assertEqual(date.today().year, 2009)

    def test_month(self):
        self.assertEqual(date.today().month, 6)

    def test_day(self):
        self.assertEqual(date.today().day, 12)

class second_tests(TestCase):
    def test_isoformat(self):
        self.assertEqual(date.today().isoformat(), '2009-06-12')
```

3. Notice that there are two `TestCase` classes in this module. Using pure unittest, we'd have to duplicate the fixture code in each of those classes.

4. Go ahead and run the tests by moving to the directory that contains the `tests` directory and typing:

```
$ nosetests
```

5. Nose will recognize tests as a directory that may contain tests (because of the directory name), find the `module_fixtures_tests.py` file, run the `setup` function, run all of the tests, and then run the `teardown` function. There won't be much to see though, aside from a simple report of how many tests passed.

What just happened?

We saved ourselves some time and effort by using a second 'layer' of test fixtures, which wrap around entire test modules instead of single test methods. By doing this, we saved ourselves from duplicating the fixture code inside every test class in the module, but this savings comes with a cost. The setup and teardown aren't run before and after each test, as normal test fixtures are. Instead, all of the tests in the module happen between a single module-level setup/teardown pair, which means that if a test does something that affects the environment created by the setup function, it won't be undone before the next test runs. In other words, isolation of tests is not guaranteed with respect to the environment created by a module-level fixture.

Now we'll expand on the previous *Time for action* by including a package-level test fixture. Like the module-level test fixture, this is a labor-saving feature of Nose.

Time for action – creating a package fixture

Now we'll create a fixture that wraps around all the test modules in an entire package.

1. Add a new file called `__init__.py` in the `tests` directory that we created in the last *Time for action* section. (That's two underbars, the word 'init, and two more underbars). The presence of this file tells Python that the directory is a package. Place the following code inside of `__init__.py` in the `tests` directory:

```
from mocker import Mocker
from datetime import datetime

mocker = Mocker()

def setup():
    fake_datetime = mocker.replace(datetime)
    fake_datetime.now()
    mocker.result(datetime(year = 2009, month = 6, day = 12,
                           hour = 10, minute = 15, second = 5))
    mocker.count(1, None)
```

```
        mocker.replay()
def teardown():
        mocker.restore()
        mocker.verify()
```

 It's fairly common that __init__.py files are completely empty, but they're a perfect place for code that is general to an entire package, so that's where Nose looks for a package-level fixture.

2. Add a new file called `package_fixtures_tests.py` to the `tests` directory, with the following contents:

```
from unittest import TestCase
from datetime import datetime

class first_tests(TestCase):
    def test_year(self):
        self.assertEqual(datetime.now().year, 2009)

    def test_month(self):
        self.assertEqual(datetime.now().month, 6)

    def test_day(self):
        self.assertEqual(datetime.now().day, 12)

    def test_hour(self):
        self.assertEqual(datetime.now().hour, 10)

    def test_minute(self):
        self.assertEqual(datetime.now().minute, 15)

    def test_second(self):
        self.assertEqual(datetime.now().second, 5)
```

3. Add the following code to the already-existing `module_fixtures_tests.py` (We could place it in its own file too. The point is placing it in a separate module from the tests in step 2, for you to see that the package test fixture is in place):

```
from datetime import datetime
class third_tests(TestCase):
    def test_isoformat(self):
        self.assertEqual(datetime.now().isoformat(),
                         '2009-06-12T10:15:05')
```

4. Go ahead an run the tests again. (You won't see much output, but that means everything worked) Go to the directory containing `tests` and run the following:

```
$ nosetests
```

What just happened?

We worked with yet another layer of test fixture, this time wrapping around all of the test modules in the `tests` directory. As you can see from looking at the code that we just wrote, the environment created by the package-level test fixture is available in every test in every module in the package.

Like module-level test fixtures, package-level test fixtures can be a big labor-saving shortcut. However, they don't provide you with the protection against communication between tests that *real* test-level fixtures do.

Nose's own testing framework

Nose supports two new kinds of tests: stand-alone test functions and non-TestCase test classes. It finds these tests by using the same pattern matching that it uses to find test modules. When looking through a module whose name matches the pattern, any functions or classes whose names also match the pattern, are assumed to be tests.

Time for action – using Nose-specific tests

We'll write a few tests that demonstrate Nose's support for test functions and non-TestCase test classes.

1. Create a file called `nose_specific_tests.py` with the following contents:

```
import sys
from sqlite3 import connect
class grouped_tests:
    def setup(self):
        self.connection = connect(':memory:')
        cursor = self.connection.cursor()
        cursor.execute('create table test (a, b, c)')
        cursor.execute('''insert into test (a, b, c)
                          values (1, 2, 3)''')
        self.connection.commit()
    def teardown(self):
        self.connection.close()
    def test_update(self):
        cursor = self.connection.cursor()
        cursor.execute('update test set b = 7 where a = 1')
    def test_select(self):
        cursor = self.connection.cursor()
        cursor.execute('select * from test limit 1')
        assert cursor.fetchone() == (1, 2, 3)
```

2. Now add the following text to the same file, *outside* of the grouped_tests class:

```
def platform_setup():
    sys.platform = 'test platform'

def platform_teardown():
    global sys
    sys = reload(sys)

def standalone_test():
    assert sys.platform == 'test platform'

standalone_test.setup = platform_setup
standalone_test.teardown = platform_teardown
```

3. Run the tests, although as usual you don't want to see any output beyond a report of how many tests were executed:

```
$ nosetests
```

What just happened?

The grouped_tests class contains a test fixture (the setup and teardown methods) and two tests, but it's not a unittest TestCase class. Nose recognized it as a test class because its name follows the same pattern that Nose looks for, when it checks module names to find test modules. It then looks through the class for a test fixture (and any test methods), and runs them appropriately.

Since the class isn't a TestCase, the tests don't have access to any of unittest's assert methods; Nose considers such a test to pass unless it raises an exception. Python has an assert statement that raises an exception if its expression is false, which is helpful for this sort of thing. It's not as nice as assertEqual, but it does the job in many cases.

We wrote another test in the function standalone_test. Like grouped_tests, standalone_test is recognized as a test by Nose because its name matches the same pattern that Nose uses to search for test modules. Nose runs standalone_test as a test, and reports a failure if it raises an exception.

We were able to attach a test fixture to standalone_test, by setting its setup and teardown attributes to a pair of functions that we defined for that purpose. As usual, the setup function gets executed before the test function and the teardown function gets run after.

Summary

We learned a lot in this chapter about the Nose testing meta-framework.

Specifically, we covered:

- How Nose finds the files that contain tests, and how you can adapt the process to fit into your organization scheme
- How to run all of your tests with Nose, whether they are doctest, unittest, or nose-specific tests
- How Nose enhances the other frameworks with additional support for test fixtures
- How to use Nose's test functions and non-TestCase test classes

Now that we've learned about Nose and running all of our tests easily, we're ready to tackle a complete test-driven project—which is the topic of the next chapter.

7

Developing a Test-Driven Project

In this chapter, we won't talk about new techniques for testing in Python, neither will we spend much time talking about the philosophy of testing. Instead, what we'll do is walk step-by-step through a record of an actual development process. Your humble and sadly fallible author has memorialized his mistakes—and the ways that testing helped him fix them—while developing part of a personal scheduling program.

In this chapter, we shall:

- ◆ Write a testable specification
- ◆ Write unit tests
- ◆ Write code that complies with the specification and unit tests
- ◆ Use the testable specification and unit tests to help debug

You'll be prompted to design and build your own module as you read through this chapter, so that you can walk through your own process as well.

Writing the specification

As usual, the process starts with a written specification. The specification is a doctest, (which we learned about in Chapters 2 and 3), so the computer can use it to check the implementation. The specification isn't strictly a set of unit tests though; the discipline of unit testing has been sacrificed (for the moment) in exchange for making the document more accessible to a human reader. That's a common trade-off, and it's fine as long as you make up for it by also writing unit tests covering the code.

The goal of the project is to make a Python package capable of representing personal time management information.

The following code goes in a file called docs/outline.txt:

```
This project is a personal scheduling system intended to keep track of
a single person's schedule and activities. The system will store and
display two kinds of schedule information: activities and statuses.
Activities and statuses both support a protocol which allows them to
be checked for overlap with another object supporting the protocol.
>>> from planner.data import activities, statuses
>>> from datetime import datetime
```

Activities and statuses are stored in schedules, to which they can be added and removed.

```
>>> from planner.data import schedules
>>> activity = activities('test activity',
...                          datetime(year=2009, month=6, day=1,
...                                   hour=10, minute=15),
...                          datetime(year=2009, month=6, day=1,
...                                   hour=12, minute=30))
>>> duplicate_activity = activities('test activity',
...                          datetime(year=2009, month=6, day=1,
...                                   hour=10, minute=15),
...                          datetime(year=2009, month=6, day=1,
...                                   hour=12, minute=30))
>>> status = statuses('test status',
...                      datetime(year=2009, month=7, day=1,
...                               hour=10, minute=15),
...                      datetime(year=2009, month=7, day=1,
...                               hour=12, minute=30))
>>> schedule = schedules()
>>> schedule.add(activity)
>>> schedule.add(status)
>>> status in schedule
True
>>> activity in schedule
True
>>> duplicate_activity in schedule
True
>>> schedule.remove(activity)
>>> schedule.remove(status)
>>> status in schedule
False
>>> activity in schedule
```

```
False
```

Activities represent tasks that the person must actively engage in, and they are therefore mutually exclusive: no person can have two activities that overlap the same period of time.

```
>>> activity1 = activities('test activity 1',
...                         datetime(year=2009, month=6, day=1,
...                                  hour=9, minute=5),
...                         datetime(year=2009, month=6, day=1,
...                                  hour=12, minute=30))
>>> activity2 = activities('test activity 2',
...                         datetime(year=2009, month=6, day=1,
...                                  hour=10, minute=15),
...                         datetime(year=2009, month=6, day=1,
...                                  hour=13, minute=30))
>>> schedule = schedules()
>>> schedule.add(activity1)
>>> schedule.add(activity2) # doctest:+ELLIPSIS
Traceback (most recent call last):
schedule_error: "test activity 2" overlaps with "test activity 1"
```

Statuses represent tasks that a person engages in passively, and so can overlap with each other and with activities.

```
>>> activity1 = activities('test activity 1',
...                         datetime(year=2009, month=6, day=1,
...                                  hour=9, minute=5),
...                         datetime(year=2009, month=6, day=1,
...                                  hour=12, minute=30))
>>> status1 = statuses('test status 1',
...                     datetime(year=2009, month=6, day=1,
...                              hour=10, minute=15),
...                     datetime(year=2009, month=6, day=1,
...                              hour=13, minute=30))
>>> status2 = statuses('test status 2',
...                     datetime(year=2009, month=6, day=1,
...                              hour=8, minute=45),
...                     datetime(year=2009, month=6, day=1,
...                              hour=15, minute=30))
>>> schedule = schedules()
>>> schedule.add(activity1)
>>> schedule.add(status1)
>>> schedule.add(status2)
>>> activity1 in schedule
True
>>> status1 in schedule
```

```
True
>>> status2 in schedule
True
```

Schedules can be saved to a sqlite database, and they can be reloaded from that stored state.

```
>>> from planner.persistence import file
>>> storage = file(':memory:')
>>> schedule.store(storage)
>>> newsched = schedules.load(storage)
>>> schedule == newsched
True
```

This doctest will serve as a testable specification for my project, which means that it will be the foundation stone on which all of my other tests (and my program code) will be built on. Let's look at each section in more detail:

This project is a personal scheduling system intended to keep track of a single person's schedule and activities. The system will store and display two kinds of schedule information: activities and statuses. Activities and statuses both support a protocol which allows them to be checked for overlap with another object supporting the protocol.

```
>>> from planner.data import activities, statuses
>>> from datetime import datetime
```

The above code consists of some introductory English text and a couple of import statements that bring in code that we need for these tests. By doing so, they also tell us about some of the structure of the `planner` package. Specifically, they tell us that it contains a module called `data`, which defines activities and statuses.

```
>>> from planner.data import schedules
>>> activity = activities('test activity',
...                       datetime(year=2009, month=6, day=1,
...                                hour=10, minute=15),
...                       datetime(year=2009, month=6, day=1,
...                                hour=12, minute=30))
>>> duplicate_activity = activities('test activity',
...                       datetime(year=2009, month=6, day=1,
...                                hour=10, minute=15),
...                       datetime(year=2009, month=6, day=1,
...                                hour=12, minute=30))
>>> status = statuses('test status',
...                   datetime(year=2009, month=7, day=1,
...                            hour=10, minute=15),
...                   datetime(year=2009, month=7, day=1,
...                            hour=12, minute=30))
```

```
>>> schedule = schedules()
>>> schedule.add(activity)
>>> schedule.add(status)
>>> status in schedule
True
>>> activity in schedule
True
>>> duplicate_activity in schedule
True
>>> schedule.remove(activity)
>>> schedule.remove(status)
>>> status in schedule
False
>>> activity in schedule
False
```

The above tests describe some of the desired behavior of `schedules` for `activities` and `statuses`. According to these tests, `schedules` must accept `activities` and `statuses` as parameters of its `add` and `remove` methods. Once they're added, the `in` operator must return `True` for an object until it is removed. Furthermore, two `activities` that have the same parameters must be treated as the same object by `schedules`.

```
>>> activity1 = activities('test activity 1',
...                         datetime(year=2009, month=6, day=1,
...                                  hour=9, minute=5),
...                         datetime(year=2009, month=6, day=1,
...                                  hour=12, minute=30))
>>> activity2 = activities('test activity 2',
...                         datetime(year=2009, month=6, day=1,
...                                  hour=10, minute=15),
...                         datetime(year=2009, month=6, day=1,
...                                  hour=13, minute=30))
>>> schedule = schedules()
>>> schedule.add(activity1)
>>> schedule.add(activity2) # doctest:+ELLIPSIS
Traceback (most recent call last):
schedule_error: "test activity 2" overlaps with "test activity 1"
```

The above test code describes what should happen when overlapping activities are added to a schedule. Specifically, a `schedule_error` should be raised.

```
>>> activity1 = activities('test activity 1',
...                         datetime(year=2009, month=6, day=1,
...                                  hour=9, minute=5),
...                         datetime(year=2009, month=6, day=1,
...                                  hour=12, minute=30))
```

```
>>> status1 = statuses('test status 1',
...                     datetime(year=2009, month=6, day=1,
...                              hour=10, minute=15),
...                     datetime(year=2009, month=6, day=1,
...                              hour=13, minute=30))
>>> status2 = statuses('test status 2',
...                     datetime(year=2009, month=6, day=1,
...                              hour=8, minute=45),
...                     datetime(year=2009, month=6, day=1,
...                              hour=15, minute=30))
>>> schedule = schedules()
>>> schedule.add(activity1)
>>> schedule.add(status1)
>>> schedule.add(status2)
>>> activity1 in schedule
True
>>> status1 in schedule
True
>>> status2 in schedule
True
```

The above test code describes what should happen when overlapping statuses are added to a schedule: the schedule should accept them. Furthermore, if a status and an activity overlap, they can still both be added.

```
>>> from planner.persistence import file
>>> storage = file(':memory:')
>>> schedule.store(storage)
>>> newsched = schedules.load(storage)
>>> schedule == newsched
True
```

The above code describes how schedule storage should work. It also tells us that the planner **package needs to contain a** persistence **module, which in turn should contain** file.

Time for action – what are you going to do?

It's time for you to come up with a project of your own, something that you can work on by yourself; we step through the development process:

1. Think of a project of approximately the same complexity as the one described in this chapter. It should be a single module or a few modules in a single package.

2. Imagine that the project is already done, and you need to write a description of what you've done, along with a little bit of demonstration code. Then go ahead and write your description and demo code in the form of a doctest file.

3. As you're writing the doctest file, look out for places where your original idea has to change a little bit to make the demo easier to write, or work better. When you find such cases, pay attention to them! At this stage, it's better to change the idea a little bit and save yourself effort all through the process.

What just happened?

We've got testable specifications for moderately-sized projects, now. These will help us to write unit tests and code, and they'll give us a sense of how complete the project is, as a whole.

In addition, the process of writing code into the doctest gave us a chance to test-drive our ideas. We've probably improved our projects a little bit by using them in a concrete manner, even though the project implementation is still merely imaginary.

Once again, it's important that we have written these tests *before* writing the code that they will test. By writing the tests first, we give ourselves a touchstone that we can use to judge how well our code conforms to what we intended. If we write the code first, and then the tests, all we end up doing is enshrining what the code actually does—as opposed to what we meant for it to do—into the tests.

Writing initial unit tests

Since the specification doesn't contain unit tests, there's still a need for unit tests before the coding of the module can begin. The `planner.data` classes are the first target for implementation, so they're the first ones to get tests.

Activities and statuses are defined to be very similar, so their test modules are also similar. They're not identical though, and they're not required to have any particular inheritance relationship, so the tests remain distinct.

The following tests are in `tests/test_activities.py`:

```python
from unittest import TestCase
from mocker import MockerTestCase
from planner.data import activities, task_error
from datetime import datetime

class constructor_tests(TestCase):
    def test_valid(self):
        activity = activities('activity name',
                              datetime(year=2007, month=9, day=11),
                              datetime(year=2008, month=4, day=27))

        self.assertEqual(activity.name, 'activity name')
        self.assertEqual(activity.begins,
                         datetime(year = 2007, month = 9, day = 11))
        self.assertEqual(activity.ends,
                         datetime(year = 2008, month = 4, day = 27))

    def test_backwards_times(self):
        self.assertRaises(task_error,
                          activities,
                          'activity name',
                          datetime(year=2008, month=4, day=27),
                          datetime(year=2007, month=9, day=11))

    def test_too_short(self):
        self.assertRaises(task_error,
                          activities,
                          'activity name',
                          datetime(year = 2008, month = 4, day = 27,
                                   hour = 7, minute = 15),
                          datetime(year = 2008, month = 4, day = 27,
                                   hour = 7, minute = 15))

class utility_tests(TestCase):
    def test_repr(self):
        activity = activities('activity name',
                              datetime(year=2007, month=9, day=11),
                              datetime(year=2008, month=4, day=27))

        expected = "<activity name 2007-09-11T00:00:00 2008-04-27T00:00:00>"

        self.assertEqual(repr(activity), expected)

class exclusivity_tests(TestCase):
    def test_excludes(self):
        activity = activities('activity name',
                              datetime(year=2007, month=9, day=11),
```

```
                                 datetime(year=2007, month=10, day=6))
        # Any activity should exclude any other activity
        self.assertTrue(activity.excludes(activity))

        # Anything not known to be excluded should be included
        self.assertFalse(activity.excludes(None))
class overlap_tests(MockerTestCase):
    def setUp(self):
        pseudo = self.mocker.mock()

        pseudo.begins
        self.mocker.result(datetime(year=2007, month=10, day=7))
        self.mocker.count(0, None)

        pseudo.ends
        self.mocker.result(datetime(year=2008, month=2, day=5))
        self.mocker.count(0, None)

        self.other = pseudo

        self.mocker.replay()

    def test_overlap_before(self):
        activity = activities('activity name',
                              datetime(year=2007, month=9, day=11),
                              datetime(year=2007, month=10, day=6))

        self.assertFalse(activity.overlaps(self.other))

    def test_overlap_begin(self):
        activity = activities('activity name',
                              datetime(year=2007, month=8, day=11),
                              datetime(year=2007, month=11, day=27))

        self.assertTrue(activity.overlaps(self.other))

    def test_overlap_end(self):
        activity = activities('activity name',
                              datetime(year=2008, month=1, day=11),
                              datetime(year=2008, month=4, day=16))

        self.assertTrue(activity.overlaps(self.other))

    def test_overlap_inner(self):
        activity = activities('activity name',
                              datetime(year=2007, month=10, day=11),
                              datetime(year=2008, month=1, day=27))

        self.assertTrue(activity.overlaps(self.other))

    def test_overlap_outer(self):
        activity = activities('activity name',
                              datetime(year=2007, month=8, day=12),
```

```
                                    datetime(year=2008, month=3, day=15))
            self.assertTrue(activity.overlaps(self.other))
    def test_overlap_after(self):
        activity = activities('activity name',
                                    datetime(year=2008, month=2, day=6),
                                    datetime(year=2008, month=4, day=27))
            self.assertFalse(activity.overlaps(self.other))
```

Let's take a look at each section of the above unit test code:

```
    def test_valid(self):
        activity = activities('activity name',
                                    datetime(year=2007, month=9, day=11),
                                    datetime(year=2008, month=4, day=27))

            self.assertEqual(activity.name, 'activity name')
            self.assertEqual(activity.begins,
                            datetime(year = 2007, month = 9, day = 11))
            self.assertEqual(activity.ends,
                            datetime(year = 2008, month = 4, day = 27))
```

The `test_valid` method checks that the constructor works correctly when all of the parameters are correct. This is an important test, because it defines what correct behavior in the normal case should be. We need more tests though, to define correct behavior in abnormal situations.

```
    def test_backwards_times(self):
        self.assertRaises(task_error,
                            activities,
                            'activity name',
                            datetime(year=2008, month=4, day=27),
                            datetime(year=2007, month=9, day=11))
```

Here, we'll make sure that you can't create an activity that ends before it begins. That doesn't make any sense, and could easily throw off assumptions made during the implementation.

```
    def test_too_short(self):
        self.assertRaises(task_error,
                            activities,
                            'activity name',
                            datetime(year = 2008, month = 4, day = 27,
                                    hour = 7, minute = 15),
                            datetime(year = 2008, month = 4, day = 27,
                                    hour = 7, minute = 15))
```

We don't want extremely short activities either. In the real world, an activity that takes no time is meaningless, so we have a test here to make sure that such things are not allowed.

```
class utility_tests(TestCase):
    def test_repr(self):
        activity = activities('activity name',
                              datetime(year=2007, month=9, day=11),
                              datetime(year=2008, month=4, day=27))
        expected = "<activity name 2007-09-11T00:00:00 2008-04-27T00:
00:00>"
        self.assertEqual(repr(activity), expected)
```

While `repr(activity)` isn't likely to be used in any production code paths, it's handy during development and debugging. This test defines how the text representation of an activity should look, to make sure that it contains the desired information.

```
class exclusivity_tests(TestCase):
    def test_excludes(self):
        activity = activities('activity name',
                              datetime(year=2007, month=9, day=11),
                              datetime(year=2007, month=10, day=6))
        # Any activity should exclude any other activity
        self.assertTrue(activity.excludes(activity))

        # Anything not known to be excluded should be included
        self.assertFalse(activity.excludes(None))
```

Since activities are supposed to be exclusive of each other when they overlap, we check that here. The activity obviously overlaps with itself, so the `excludes` method should return `True`. On the other hand, an activity shouldn't just assume it excludes everything, so calling `excludes` on unknown objects (such as `None`) should return `False`.

```
class overlap_tests(MockerTestCase):
    def setUp(self):
        pseudo = self.mocker.mock()

        pseudo.begins
        self.mocker.result(datetime(year=2007, month=10, day=7))
        self.mocker.count(0, None)

        pseudo.ends
        self.mocker.result(datetime(year=2008, month=2, day=5))
        self.mocker.count(0, None)

        self.other = pseudo

        self.mocker.replay()
```

Here we created a test fixture that creates a mock object which pretends to be an activity or status. We'll use this mock object (called `self.other`) in several of the following tests.

```
def test_overlap_before(self):
    activity = activities('activity name',
                          datetime(year=2007, month=9, day=11),
                          datetime(year=2007, month=10, day=6))
    self.assertFalse(activity.overlaps(self.other))
def test_overlap_begin(self):
    activity = activities('activity name',
                          datetime(year=2007, month=8, day=11),
                          datetime(year=2007, month=11, day=27))
    self.assertTrue(activity.overlaps(self.other))
def test_overlap_end(self):
    activity = activities('activity name',
                          datetime(year=2008, month=1, day=11),
                          datetime(year=2008, month=4, day=16))
    self.assertTrue(activity.overlaps(self.other))
def test_overlap_inner(self):
    activity = activities('activity name',
                          datetime(year=2007, month=10, day=11),
                          datetime(year=2008, month=1, day=27))
    self.assertTrue(activity.overlaps(self.other))
def test_overlap_outer(self):
    activity = activities('activity name',
                          datetime(year=2007, month=8, day=12),
                          datetime(year=2008, month=3, day=15))
    self.assertTrue(activity.overlaps(self.other))
def test_overlap_after(self):
    activity = activities('activity name',
                          datetime(year=2008, month=2, day=6),
                          datetime(year=2008, month=4, day=27))
    self.assertFalse(activity.overlaps(self.other))
```

These tests describe the behavior of activity overlap checking in the cases where the activity:

- Comes after the mock object
- Overlaps the end of the mock object
- Overlaps the beginning of the mock object
- Starts after the mock object and ends before it
- Starts before the mock object and ends after it

The following tests are in `tests/test_statuses.py`. Many of these are similar to the tests for `activities`. We'll concentrate on the differences:

```python
from unittest import TestCase
from mocker import MockerTestCase
from planner.data import statuses, task_error
from datetime import datetime

class constructor_tests(TestCase):
    def test_valid(self):
        status = statuses('status name',
                          datetime(year=2007, month=9, day=11),
                          datetime(year=2008, month=4, day=27))

        self.assertEqual(status.name, 'status name')
        self.assertEqual(status.begins,
                          datetime(year=2007, month=9, day=11))
        self.assertEqual(status.ends,
                          datetime(year=2008, month=4, day=27))

    def test_backwards_times(self):
        self.assertRaises(task_error,
                          statuses,
                          'status name',
                          datetime(year=2008, month=4, day=27),
                          datetime(year=2007, month=9, day=11))

    def test_too_short(self):
        self.assertRaises(task_error,
                          statuses,
                          'status name',
                          datetime(year=2008, month=4, day=27,
                                   hour=7, minute=15),
                          datetime(year=2008, month=4, day=27,
                                   hour=7, minute=15))

class utility_tests(TestCase):
    def test_repr(self):
        status = statuses('status name',
                          datetime(year=2007, month=9, day=11),
                          datetime(year=2008, month=4, day=27))

        expected = "<status name 2007-09-11T00:00:00 2008-04-27T00:00:00>"

        self.assertEqual(repr(status), expected)
```

```
class exclusivity_tests(TestCase):
    def test_excludes(self):
        status = statuses('status name',
                          datetime(year=2007, month=9, day=11),
                          datetime(year=2007, month=10, day=6))

        # A status shouldn't exclude anything
        self.assertFalse(status.excludes(status))
        self.assertFalse(status.excludes(None))

class overlap_tests(MockerTestCase):
    def setUp(self):
        pseudo = self.mocker.mock()

        pseudo.begins
        self.mocker.result(datetime(year=2007, month=10, day=7))
        self.mocker.count(1, None)

        pseudo.ends
        self.mocker.result(datetime(year=2008, month=2, day=5))
        self.mocker.count(1, None)

        self.other = pseudo

        self.mocker.replay()

    def test_overlap_before(self):
        status = statuses('status name',
                          datetime(year=2007, month=9, day=11),
                          datetime(year=2007, month=10, day=6))

        self.assertFalse(status.overlaps(self.other))

    def test_overlap_begin(self):
        status = statuses('status name',
                          datetime(year=2007, month=8, day=11),
                          datetime(year=2007, month=11, day=27))

        self.assertTrue(status.overlaps(self.other))

    def test_overlap_end(self):
        status = statuses('status name',
                          datetime(year=2008, month=1, day=11),
                          datetime(year=2008, month=4, day=16))

        self.assertTrue(status.overlaps(self.other))

    def test_overlap_inner(self):
        status = statuses('status name',
                          datetime(year=2007, month=10, day=11),
                          datetime(year=2008, month=1, day=27))

        self.assertTrue(status.overlaps(self.other))
```

```
    def test_overlap_outer(self):
        status = statuses('status name',
                          datetime(year=2007, month=8, day=12),
                          datetime(year=2008, month=3, day=15))
        self.assertTrue(status.overlaps(self.other))
    def test_overlap_after(self):
        status = statuses('status name',
                          datetime(year=2008, month=2, day=6),
                          datetime(year=2008, month=4, day=27))
        self.assertFalse(status.overlaps(self.other))
```

There's one significant area of difference between this test file and the previous one, the test_excludes method.

```
    class exclusivity_tests(TestCase):
        def test_excludes(self):
            status = statuses('status name',
                              datetime(year=2007, month=9, day=11),
                              datetime(year=2007, month=10, day=6))
            # A status shouldn't exclude anything
            self.assertFalse(status.excludes(status))
            self.assertFalse(status.excludes(None))
```

Unlike an activity, a status should never force itself to be exclusive with something else, so this test uses assertFalse, instead of assertTrue for the first assertion.

The following tests are in tests/test_schedules.py. We define several mock objects in the setUp method that behave as if they were activities or statuses. These mock objects simulate activities or statuses, and so by using them instead of real activities or statuses they allow us to check that the schedules class correctly handles events that either do or do not overlap, and that either do or do not exclude each other, all without actually using code from outside the unit being tested.

```
    from unittest import TestCase
    from mocker import MockerTestCase, ANY
    from planner.data import schedules, schedule_error
    from datetime import datetime

    class add_tests(MockerTestCase):
        def setUp(self):
            overlap_exclude = self.mocker.mock()
            overlap_exclude.overlaps(ANY)
            self.mocker.result(True)
            self.mocker.count(0, None)
            overlap_exclude.excludes(ANY)
```

```
            self.mocker.result(True)
            self.mocker.count(0, None)

            overlap_include = self.mocker.mock()
            overlap_include.overlaps(ANY)
            self.mocker.result(True)
            self.mocker.count(0, None)
            overlap_include.excludes(ANY)
            self.mocker.result(False)
            self.mocker.count(0, None)

            distinct_exclude = self.mocker.mock()
            distinct_exclude.overlaps(ANY)
            self.mocker.result(False)
            self.mocker.count(0, None)
            distinct_exclude.excludes(ANY)
            self.mocker.result(True)
            self.mocker.count(0, None)

            distinct_include = self.mocker.mock()
            distinct_include.overlaps(ANY)
            self.mocker.result(False)
            self.mocker.count(0, None)
            distinct_include.excludes(ANY)
            self.mocker.result(False)
            self.mocker.count(0, None)

            self.overlap_exclude = overlap_exclude
            self.overlap_include = overlap_include
            self.distinct_exclude = distinct_exclude
            self.distinct_include = distinct_include

            self.mocker.replay()

    def test_add_overlap_exclude(self):
        schedule = schedules()
        schedule.add(self.distinct_include)
        self.assertRaises(schedule_error,
                          schedule.add,
                          self.overlap_exclude)

    def test_add_overlap_include(self):
        schedule = schedules()
        schedule.add(self.distinct_include)
        schedule.add(self.overlap_include)

    def test_add_distinct_exclude(self):
        schedule = schedules()
        schedule.add(self.distinct_include)
        schedule.add(self.distinct_exclude)
```

```python
    def test_add_distinct_include(self):
        schedule = schedules()
        schedule.add(self.distinct_include)
        schedule.add(self.distinct_include)

    def test_add_over_overlap_exclude(self):
        schedule = schedules()
        schedule.add(self.overlap_exclude)
        self.assertRaises(schedule_error,
                          schedule.add,
                          self.overlap_include)

    def test_add_over_distinct_exclude(self):
        schedule = schedules()
        schedule.add(self.distinct_exclude)
        self.assertRaises(schedule_error,
                          schedule.add,
                          self.overlap_include)

    def test_add_over_overlap_include(self):
        schedule = schedules()
        schedule.add(self.overlap_include)
        schedule.add(self.overlap_include)

    def test_add_over_distinct_include(self):
        schedule = schedules()
        schedule.add(self.distinct_include)
        schedule.add(self.overlap_include)

class in_tests(MockerTestCase):
    def setUp(self):
        fake = self.mocker.mock()
        fake.overlaps(ANY)
        self.mocker.result(True)
        self.mocker.count(0, None)
        fake.excludes(ANY)
        self.mocker.result(True)
        self.mocker.count(0, None)

        self.fake = fake

        self.mocker.replay()

    def test_in_before_add(self):
        schedule = schedules()
        self.assertFalse(self.fake in schedule)

    def test_in_after_add(self):
        schedule = schedules()
        schedule.add(self.fake)
        self.assertTrue(self.fake in schedule)
```

Let's go over those tests section by section.

```
def setUp(self):
    overlap_exclude = self.mocker.mock()
    overlap_exclude.overlaps(ANY)
    self.mocker.result(True)
    self.mocker.count(0, None)
    overlap_exclude.excludes(ANY)
    self.mocker.result(True)
    self.mocker.count(0, None)

    overlap_include = self.mocker.mock()
    overlap_include.overlaps(ANY)
    self.mocker.result(True)
    self.mocker.count(0, None)
    overlap_include.excludes(ANY)
    self.mocker.result(False)
    self.mocker.count(0, None)

    distinct_exclude = self.mocker.mock()
    distinct_exclude.overlaps(ANY)
    self.mocker.result(False)
    self.mocker.count(0, None)
    distinct_exclude.excludes(ANY)
    self.mocker.result(True)
    self.mocker.count(0, None)

    distinct_include = self.mocker.mock()
    distinct_include.overlaps(ANY)
    self.mocker.result(False)
    self.mocker.count(0, None)
    distinct_include.excludes(ANY)
    self.mocker.result(False)
    self.mocker.count(0, None)

    self.overlap_exclude = overlap_exclude
    self.overlap_include = overlap_include
    self.distinct_exclude = distinct_exclude
    self.distinct_include = distinct_include

    self.mocker.replay()
```

We created four mock objects here: `overlap_exclude`, `overlap_include`, `distinct_exclude`, and `distinct_include`. Each of them represents a different combination of behavior of its `overlaps` method and its `excludes` method. Between these four mock objects, we have every combination of overlapping or not overlapping, and excluding or not excluding. In the following tests, we'll add various combinations of these mock objects to a schedule, and make sure it does the right things.

```python
def test_add_overlap_exclude(self):
    schedule = schedules()
    schedule.add(self.distinct_include)
    self.assertRaises(schedule_error,
                      schedule.add,
                      self.overlap_exclude)

def test_add_overlap_include(self):
    schedule = schedules()
    schedule.add(self.distinct_include)
    schedule.add(self.overlap_include)

def test_add_distinct_exclude(self):
    schedule = schedules()
    schedule.add(self.distinct_include)
    schedule.add(self.distinct_exclude)

def test_add_distinct_include(self):
    schedule = schedules()
    schedule.add(self.distinct_include)
    schedule.add(self.distinct_include)
```

These four tests cover cases, where we add a non-overlapping object to a schedule. All of them are expected to accept the non-overlapping object, except the first. In that test, we've previously added an object that claims that it does indeed overlap, and furthermore it excludes anything it overlaps. That test shows that if either the object being added or an object already in the schedule believes there's an overlap, the schedule must treat it as an overlap.

```python
def test_add_over_overlap_exclude(self):
    schedule = schedules()
    schedule.add(self.overlap_exclude)
    self.assertRaises(schedule_error,
                      schedule.add,
                      self.overlap_include)
```

In this test, we'll make sure that if an object already in the schedule overlaps a new object and claims exclusivity, then adding the new object will fail.

```
def test_add_over_distinct_exclude(self):
    schedule = schedules()
    schedule.add(self.distinct_exclude)
    self.assertRaises(schedule_error,
                      schedule.add,
                      self.overlap_include)
```

In this test, we'll make sure that even though the object already in the schedule doesn't think it overlaps with the new object, it excludes the new object because the new object thinks that there's an overlap.

```
def test_add_over_overlap_include(self):
    schedule = schedules()
    schedule.add(self.overlap_include)
    schedule.add(self.overlap_include)

def test_add_over_distinct_include(self):
    schedule = schedules()
    schedule.add(self.distinct_include)
    schedule.add(self.overlap_include)
```

These tests make sure that inclusive objects don't somehow interfere with adding each other to a schedule.

```
class in_tests(MockerTestCase):
    def setUp(self):
        fake = self.mocker.mock()
        fake.overlaps(ANY)
        self.mocker.result(True)
        self.mocker.count(0, None)
        fake.excludes(ANY)
        self.mocker.result(True)
        self.mocker.count(0, None)

        self.fake = fake

        self.mocker.replay()

    def test_in_before_add(self):
        schedule = schedules()
        self.assertFalse(self.fake in schedule)

    def test_in_after_add(self):
        schedule = schedules()
        schedule.add(self.fake)
        self.assertTrue(self.fake in schedule)
```

These two tests describe schedule behavior with respect to the `in` operator. Specifically, `in` should return `True` when the object in question is actually in the schedule.

Time for action – nailing down the specification with unit tests

A specification—even a testable specification written in doctest—is still home to a lot of ambiguities that can be ironed out with good unit tests. Add that to the fact that the specification doesn't maintain separation between different tests, and you can see that it's time for your project to gain some unit tests.

- Find some element of your project which is described in (or implied by) your specification
- Write a unit test that describes the behavior of that element when given correct input
- Write a unit test that describes the behavior of that element when given incorrect input
- Write unit tests that describe the behavior of the element at the boundaries between correct and incorrect input
- Go back to step 1 if you can find another untested part of your program.

What just happened?

It doesn't take many bullet points to describe the procedure, but this is an important process. This is where you really take what was an ill-defined idea and turn it into a precise description of what you're going to do.

The end result can be quite lengthy, which shouldn't come as much of a surprise. After all, your goal at this stage is to completely define the behavior of your project; and even without bothering yourself with the details of how that behavior is implemented, that's a lot of information.

Coding planner.data

It's time to write some code, using the specification document and the unit tests as guides. Specifically, it's time to write the `planner.data` module, which contains `statuses`, `activities`, and `schedules`.

I made a directory called `planner`, and within that directory created a file called `__init__.py`. There's no need to put anything inside `__init__.py`, but the file itself needs to exist to tell Python that the `planner` directory is a package.

The following code goes in `planner/data.py`:

```python
from datetime import timedelta

class task_error(Exception):
    pass

class schedule_error(Exception):
    pass

class _tasks:
    def __init__(self, name, begins, ends):
        if ends < begins:
            raise task_error('The begin time must precede the
                             end time')
        if ends - begins < timedelta(minutes = 5):
            raise task_error('The minimum duration is 5 minutes')
        self.name = name
        self.begins = begins
        self.ends = ends

    def excludes(self, other):
        raise NotImplemented('Abstract method. Use a child class.')

    def overlaps(self, other):
        if other.begins < self.begins:
            return other.ends > self.begins
        elif other.ends > self.ends:
            return other.begins < self.ends
        else:
            return True

    def __repr__(self):
        return ''.join(['<', self.name,
                        ' ', self.begins.isoformat(),
                        ' ', self.ends.isoformat(),
                        '>'])

class activities(_tasks):
    def excludes(self, other):
        return isinstance(other, activities)

class statuses(_tasks):
    def excludes(self, other):
        return False

class schedules:
    def __init__(self, name='schedule'):
        self.tasks = []
        self.name = name
```

```
    def add(self, task):
        for contained in self.tasks:
            if task.overlaps(contained):
                if task.exclude(contained) or contained.exclude(task):
                    raise schedule_error(task, containeed)
        self.tasks.append(task)

    def remove(self, task):
        try:
            self.tasks.remove(task)
        except ValueError:
            pass

    def __contains__(self, task):
        return task in self.tasks
```

Let's go over this section by section:

```
    class _tasks:
        def __init__(self, name, begins, ends):
            if ends < begins:
                raise task_error('The begin time must precede the end
    time')
            if ends - begins < timedelta(minutes = 5):
                raise task_error('The minimum duration is 5 minutes')
            self.name = name
            self.begins = begins
            self.ends = ends

        def excludes(self, other):
            raise NotImplemented('Abstract method. Use a child class.')

        def overlaps(self, other):
            if other.begins < self.begins:
                return other.ends > self.begins
            elif other.ends > self.ends:
                return other.begins < self.ends
            else:
                return True

        def __repr__(self):
            return ''.join(['<', self.name,
                            ' ', self.begins.isoformat(),
                            ' ', self.ends.isoformat(),
                            '>'])
```

The _tasks class here contains most of the behavior that is needed for both the activities and the statuses classes. Since so much of what they do is common to both, it makes sense to write the code once and reuse it. Only the excludes method needs to be different in each of the subclasses.

```python
class activities(_tasks):
    def excludes(self, other):
        return isinstance(other, activities)

class statuses(_tasks):
    def excludes(self, other):
        return False

class schedules:
    def __init__(self, name='schedule'):
        self.tasks = []
        self.name = name

    def add(self, task):
        for contained in self.tasks:
            if task.overlaps(contained):
                if task.exclude(contained) or contained.exclude(task):
                    raise schedule_error(task, containeed)
        self.tasks.append(task)

    def remove(self, task):
        try:
            self.tasks.remove(task)
        except ValueError:
            pass

    def __contains__(self, task):
        return task in self.tasks
```

Here we have the implementations of the classes that our tests actually require to exist. The activities and statuses classes are very simple, by virtue of inheriting from _tasks. The schedules class turns out to be pretty easy, too. But is it right? Our tests will tell us.

Using the tests to get the code right

All right, so that code looks fairly good. Unfortunately, Nose tells us there are a few problems. Actually, Nose reports quite a large number of problems, but the first ones needing to be fixed are shown below:

```
File "/home/djarb/writing/book/project/step3/docs/outline.txt", line 36, in outline.txt
Failed example:
    duplicate_activity in schedule
Expected:
    True
Got:
    False

File "/home/djarb/writing/book/project/step3/docs/outline.txt", line 61, in outline.txt
Failed example:
    schedule.add(activity2) # doctest:+ELLIPSIS
Expected:
    Traceback (most recent call last):
    schedule_error: "test activity 2" overlaps with "test activity 1"
Got:
    Traceback (most recent call last):
      File "/usr/lib64/python2.6/doctest.py", line 1241, in __run
        compileflags, 1) in test.globs
      File "<doctest outline.txt[20]>", line 1, in <module>
        schedule.add(activity2) # doctest:+ELLIPSIS
      File "/home/djarb/writing/book/project/step3/planner/data.py", line 53, in add
        if task.exclude(contained) or contained.exclude(task):
    AttributeError: activities instance has no attribute 'exclude'
```

The reason for focusing on those errors, when we have so many to choose from, is simple. A lot of the other errors seem to be derived from these. The unit tests also report problems with exclude, so we know that one isn't derived from some other error—remember that unit tests aren't influenced by each other, unlike the tests in our specification.

Fixing the code

To fix the first error, add the following code to the _tasks class in `planner/data.py`:

```
def __eq__(self, other):
    return self.name == other.name and self.begins == other.begins
    and self.ends == other.ends

def __ne__(self, other):
    return not self.__eq__(other)
```

(Beware of the wrapped line in __eq__)

As you can probably tell, that code overrides the equality comparison between two _tasks, declaring them to be equal if they have the same name, begin time and end time. That's the equality metric that's implicitly assumed by the test code.

The second error can be fixed by fixing the typographical errors in `schedules.add`:

```
def add(self, task):
    for contained in self.tasks:
        if task.overlaps(contained):
            if task.excludes(contained) or contained.
excludes(task):
                raise schedule_error(task, containeed)
    self.tasks.append(task)
```

In this case, we changed the incorrect method name `exclude` to the correct method name `excludes`. (Again, watch out for wrapped lines)

So now, I run Nose again and it breaks:

```
Traceback (most recent call last):
  File "build/bdist.linux-x86_64/egg/mocker.py", line 102, in test_method_wrapper
    result = test_method()
  File "/home/djarb/writing/book/project/step4/tests/test_schedules.py", line 94, in test_add_over_distinct_exclude
    self.overlap_include)
  File "/usr/lib64/python2.6/unittest.py", line 336, in failUnlessRaises
    callableObj(*args, **kwargs)
  File "/home/djarb/writing/book/project/step4/planner/data.py", line 60, in add
    raise schedule_error(task, containeed)
NameError: global name 'containeed' is not defined
```

Fortunately, this is an easy fix: take out the extra 'e' in 'contained':

```
                raise schedule_error(task, contained)
```

For the skeptical reader, I'm compelled to admit that, yes, that typo really did slip by until the test caught it. Sometimes tests catch boring mistakes instead of dramatic problems, typos instead of logic errors. It doesn't really matter, because either way the test is helping you make your code more solid, more reliable, and better.

So now, when I run Nose it breaks:

```
Failed example:
    schedule.add(activity2) # doctest:+ELLIPSIS
Expected:
    Traceback (most recent call last):
    schedule_error: "test activity 2" overlaps with "test activity 1"
Got:
    Traceback (most recent call last):
      File "/usr/lib64/python2.6/doctest.py", line 1241, in __run
        compileflags, 1) in test.globs
      File "<doctest outline.txt[20]>", line 1, in <module>
        schedule.add(activity2) # doctest:+ELLIPSIS
      File "/home/djarb/writing/book/project/step4/planner/data.py", line 60, in add
        raise schedule_error(task, contained)
    schedule_error: (<test activity 2 2009-06-01T10:15:00 2009-06-01T13:30:00>, <test activity 1 2009-06-01T09:05:00 2009-06-01T12:30:00>
```

Okay, fine, this is easy to fix too. The error is just formatted wrongly. Fix that by replacing the 'raise' in `schedules.add`:

```
            raise schedule_error('"%s" overlaps with "%s"' %
                                 (task.name, contained.name))
```

This time when I run Nose, it tells me that my unit test is broken:

```
Traceback (most recent call last):
  File "build/bdist.linux-x86_64/egg/mocker.py", line 102, in test_method_wrapper
    result = test_method()
  File "/home/djarb/writing/book/project/step4/tests/test_schedules.py", line 94, in test_add_over_distinct_exclude
    self.overlap_include)
  File "/usr/lib64/python2.6/unittest.py", line 336, in failUnlessRaises
    callableObj(*args, **kwargs)
  File "/home/djarb/writing/book/project/step4/planner/data.py", line 61, in add
    (task.name, contained.name))
  File "build/bdist.linux-x86_64/egg/mocker.py", line 1055, in __getattribute__
    return self.__mocker_act__("getattr", (name,))
  File "build/bdist.linux-x86_64/egg/mocker.py", line 1039, in __mocker_act__
    raise MatchError(str(exception))
MatchError: [Mocker] Unexpected expression: overlap_include.name
```

Specifically, it's telling me that my mockups of activities and statuses are missing the name attribute. This too is simply fixed by changing the setUp method of add_tests in tests/test_schedules.py:

```
def setUp(self):
    overlap_exclude = self.mocker.mock()
    overlap_exclude.overlaps(ANY)
    self.mocker.result(True)
    self.mocker.count(0, None)
    overlap_exclude.excludes(ANY)
    self.mocker.result(True)
    self.mocker.count(0, None)
    overlap_exclude.name
    self.mocker.result('overlap_exclude')
    self.mocker.count(0, None)

    overlap_include = self.mocker.mock()
    overlap_include.overlaps(ANY)
    self.mocker.result(True)
    self.mocker.count(0, None)
    overlap_include.excludes(ANY)
    self.mocker.result(False)
    self.mocker.count(0, None)
    overlap_include.name
    self.mocker.result('overlap_include')
    self.mocker.count(0, None)

    distinct_exclude = self.mocker.mock()
    distinct_exclude.overlaps(ANY)
    self.mocker.result(False)
    self.mocker.count(0, None)
    distinct_exclude.excludes(ANY)
    self.mocker.result(True)
    self.mocker.count(0, None)
    distinct_exclude.name
```

```
self.mocker.result('distinct_exclude')
self.mocker.count(0, None)

distinct_include = self.mocker.mock()
distinct_include.overlaps(ANY)
self.mocker.result(False)
self.mocker.count(0, None)
distinct_include.excludes(ANY)
self.mocker.result(False)
self.mocker.count(0, None)
distinct_include.name
self.mocker.result('distinct_include')
self.mocker.count(0, None)

self.overlap_exclude = overlap_exclude
self.overlap_include = overlap_include
self.distinct_exclude = distinct_exclude
self.distinct_include = distinct_include

self.mocker.replay()
```

Having fixed that, Nose still reports errors, but all of them have to do with persistence. Those errors aren't surprising, because there's no persistence implementation yet.

Time for action – writing and debugging code

The basic procedure (as we've discussed before), is to write some code and run the tests to find problems with the code, and repeat. When you come across an error that isn't covered by an existing test, you write a new test and continue the process.

1. Write code that ought to satisfy at least some of your tests

2. Run your tests. If you used it when we talked about it in previous chapters, you should be able to run everything simply by executing:

   ```
   $ nosetests
   ```

3. If there are errors in the code you've already written, use the test output to help you locate and identity them. Once you understand the bugs, try to fix them and then go back to step 2.

4. Once you've fixed all the errors in the code you've written, and if your project isn't complete, choose some new tests to concentrate on and go back to step 1.

What just happened?

Enough iterations on this procedure leads you to having a complete and tested project. Of course, the real task is more difficult than simply saying "it will work," but in the end, it will work. You will produce a codebase that you can be confident in. It will also be an easier process than it would have been without the tests.

Your project may be done, but there's still more to do on the personal scheduler. At this stage of the chapter, I haven't finished going through the writing and debugging process. It's time to do that.

Writing persistence tests

Since I don't have any actual unit tests for the persistence code yet, I'll start off by making some. In the process, I have to figure how persistence will actually work. The following code goes in `tests/test_persistence.py`:

```
from unittest import TestCase
from mocker import MockerTestCase
from planner.persistence import file

class test_file(TestCase):
    def test_basic(self):
        storage = file(':memory:')
        storage.store_object('tag1', ('some object',))
        self.assertEqual(tuple(storage.load_objects('tag1')),
                         (('some object',),))

    def test_multiple_tags(self):
        storage = file(':memory:')

        storage.store_object('tag1', 'A')
        storage.store_object('tag2', 'B')
        storage.store_object('tag1', 'C')
        storage.store_object('tag1', 'D')
        storage.store_object('tag3', 'E')
        storage.store_object('tag3', 'F')

        self.assertEqual(set(storage.load_objects('tag1')),
                         set(['A', 'C', 'D']))

        self.assertEqual(set(storage.load_objects('tag2')),
                         set(['B']))

        self.assertEqual(set(storage.load_objects('tag3')),
                         set(['E', 'F']))
```

Looking at each of the important sections of the test code, we see the following:

```
def test_basic(self):
    storage = file(':memory:')
    storage.store_object('tag1', ('some object',))
    self.assertEqual(tuple(storage.load_objects('tag1')),
                     (('some object',),))
```

The `test_basic` test creates a `storage`, stores a single object under the name `tag1`, and then loads that object back from storage and checks that it is equal to the original object.

```
def test_multiple_tags(self):
    storage = file(':memory:')

    storage.store_object('tag1', 'A')
    storage.store_object('tag2', 'B')
    storage.store_object('tag1', 'C')
    storage.store_object('tag1', 'D')
    storage.store_object('tag3', 'E')
    storage.store_object('tag3', 'F')

    self.assertEqual(set(storage.load_objects('tag1')),
                     set(['A', 'C', 'D']))
    self.assertEqual(set(storage.load_objects('tag2')),
                     set(['B']))
    self.assertEqual(set(storage.load_objects('tag3')),
                     set(['E', 'F']))
```

The `test_multiple_tags` test creates a storage, and then stores multiple objects in it, some with duplicate tags. It then checks that the storage keeps all of the objects with a given tag, and returns all of them on request.

In other words, a persistence file is a multimap from string keys to object values.

Writing persistence code

Now that there are at least basic unit tests covering the persistence mechanism, it's time to write the persistence code itself. The following goes in `planner/persistence.py`:

```
import sqlite3
from cPickle import loads, dumps

class file:
    def __init__(self, path):
        self.connection = sqlite3.connect(path)

        try:
```

```
        self.connection.execute("""
            create table objects (tag, pickle)
        """)
    except sqlite3.OperationalError:
        pass
def store_object(self, tag, object):
    self.connection.execute('insert into objects values (?, ?)',
                            (tag, dumps(object)))
def load_objects(self, tag):
    cursor = self.connection.execute("""
            select pickle from objects where tag like ?
        """, (tag,))
    return [loads(row[0]) for row in cursor]
```

The `store_object` method runs a short SQL statement to store the object into a database field. The object serialization is handled by the `dumps` function from the `cPickle` module.

The `load_object` method uses SQL to query the database for the serialized version of every object stored under a given tag, and then uses `cPickle.loads` to transform those serializations into real objects for it to return.

Now I run Nose to find out what's broken:

```
Traceback (most recent call last):
  File "/home/djarb/writing/book/project/step5/tests/test_persistence.py", line 9, in test_basic
    self.assertEqual(tuple(storage.load_objects('tag1')),
  File "/home/djarb/writing/book/project/step5/planner/persistence.py", line 23, in load_objects
    return [loads(row[0]) for row in cursor]
TypeError: loads() argument 1 must be string, not unicode
```

I forgot that `sqlite` returns text data as unicode. Pickle is understandably unwilling to work with a Unicode string: it expects a byte string, and the correct way to interpret Unicode as a byte string is ambiguous. This can be solved by telling `sqlite` to store the pickled object as a BLOB (Binary Large Object). Modify the `store_object` and `load_objects` methods of `file` in `planner/persistence.py`:

```
def store_object(self, tag, object):
    self.connection.execute('insert into objects values (?, ?)',
                            (tag, sqlite3.Binary(dumps(object))))
def load_objects(self, tag):
    cursor = self.connection.execute("""
            select pickle from objects where tag like ?
        """, (tag,))
    return [loads(str(row[0])) for row in cursor]
```

Now Nose is saying that the schedules class doesn't have `store` and `load` methods, which is true. Furthermore, there aren't any unit tests that check those methods... the only error is coming from the specification doctest. Time to write some more unit tests in `tests/test_schedules.py`:

```python
from mocker import MockerTestCase, ANY, IN
...
class store_load_tests(MockerTestCase):
    def setUp(self):
        fake_tasks = []
        for i in range(50):
            fake_task = self.mocker.mock()
            fake_task.overlaps(ANY)
            self.mocker.result(False)
            self.mocker.count(0, None)
            fake_task.name
            self.mocker.result('fake %d' % i)
            self.mocker.count(0, None)
            fake_tasks.append(fake_task)

        self.tasks = fake_tasks

    def test_store(self):
        fake_file = self.mocker.mock()

        fake_file.store_object('test_schedule', IN(self.tasks))
        self.mocker.count(len(self.tasks))

        self.mocker.replay()

        schedule = schedules('test_schedule')
        for task in self.tasks:
            schedule.add(task)

        schedule.store(fake_file)

    def test_load(self):
        fake_file = self.mocker.mock()

        fake_file.load_objects('test_schedule')
        self.mocker.result(self.tasks)
        self.mocker.count(1)

        self.mocker.replay()

        schedule = schedules.load(fake_file, 'test_schedule')

        self.assertEqual(set(schedule.tasks),
                         set(self.tasks))
```

Now that I have some tests to check against, it's time to write the `store` and `load` methods of the `schedules` class in `planner/data.py`:

```python
def store(self, storage):
    for task in self.tasks:
        storage.store_object(self.name, task)

@staticmethod
def load(storage, name = 'schedule'):
    value = schedules(name)

    for task in storage.load_objects(name):
        value.add(task)

    return value
```

The `@staticmethod` notation means that you can call `load` without first creating an instance of `schedules`. Notice that the `load` method does not receive a `self` parameter.

The `@` syntax for function decorators was introduced in Python 2.4. In earlier versions back to Python 2.2, you could instead write `load = staticmethod(load)` after the method definition, which means the same thing. Before Python 2.2, there was no `staticmethod` function: the easiest way to do static "methods" was to write one as a standalone function in the same module.

This new bunch of tests and code allows us to save and restore schedules from files, and clears up most of the remaining test failures. The `planner` package is nearly finished!

Finishing up

Now, Nose only reports one failed test, the check to see whether the original `schedules` instance and the one loaded from the file are equal. The problem here is that, once again, there's a need to redefine what it means to be equal.

That can be fixed by adding the following to the definition of `schedules` in `planner/data.py`:

```python
def __eq__(self, other):
    if len(self.tasks) != len(other.tasks):
        return False

    left_tasks = list(self.tasks)
    left_tasks.sort(key = (lambda task: task.begins))
    right_tasks = list(other.tasks)
    right_tasks.sort(key = (lambda task: task.begins))
```

```
        return tuple(left_tasks) == tuple(right_tasks)
    def __ne__(self, other):
        return not self.__eq__(other)
```

 The key parameter of sort was added in Python 2.4. Prior to that version, doing such a sort would have looked like left_tasks.sort(cmp = (lambda t1, t2: cmp(t1.begins, t2.begins))).

These methods define equality between schedules to be when they contain exactly the same tasks, and define inequality to be whenever they aren't equal (It may sound silly to have to define inequality that way, but it turns out that there actually are some situations where you'd want to define it differently).

Now, the tests all pass. There's something worth paying attention to though, in the way that they pass. Specifically, a couple of them are very slow. A little investigation reveals that the slow tests are the ones that deal with schedules that contain a larger number of tasks. That reveals something very important: the schedules implementation is now conformant with the tests and specifications, but it stores and organizes data in a naïve way, and so it doesn't scale up well.

Now that there is a working implementation, well covered by unit tests, the time is ripe for optimization.

Pop quiz – test-driven development

1. I didn't follow unit testing discipline when I wrote my testable specification. What did I have to do because of that, which I wouldn't have had to do otherwise? Was it wrong to choose that path?

2. Is it desirable to minimize the number of times you run your tests?

3. If you start writing code before you write any tests, what opportunities have you lost?

Have a go hero

You worked through your own project, and we worked through a project together. Now it's time to try something completely on your own. I'll give you a little help coming up with a goal, but from there on out, it's your time to shine.

A `Skip list` is another dictionary-like data structure. You can find quite a bit of information about them on Wikipedia at `http://en.wikipedia.org/wiki/Skip_list`. Using that information (and any other references you can find, if you feel like it) and the test-driven process, write your own skip list module.

Summary

In this chapter, we looked at how to apply the skills covered in earlier parts of this book. We did this by stepping through a recording of your humble author's actual process in writing a package. At the same time, you had the chance to work through your own project, making your own decisions, and designing your own tests. You've taken the lead in a test-driven project, and you should be able to do it again whenever you want.

Now that we've covered the heart of Python testing, we're ready to talk about testing web-based user interfaces with Python and Twill—which is the topic of the next chapter.

8
Testing Web Application Frontends using Twill

We haven't talked at all about testing user interfaces. Mostly because graphical user interfaces are not very amenable to being checked by automated testing tools (it can be difficult to feed input to the system and difficult to disentangle all of the units involved). However, web applications are an exception to that rule, and their importance keeps increasing.

In this chapter, we shall:

◆ Learn to use Twill to script interactions with web sites

◆ Learn how run Twill scripts from inside a testing framework

◆ Learn how to integrate Twill operations directly into unittest tests

So let's get on with it!

Installing Twill

You can find Twill in the Python Package Index at `http://pypi.python.org/pypi/twill/`. At the time of writing, the latest version can be directly downloaded from `http://darcs.idyll.org/~t/projects/twill-0.9.tar.gz`.

Windows users will need to use an archiving program which understands Tar and GZip formats, such as 7-Zip (`http://www.7-zip.org/`) to extract the files.

Once you have the files unpacked, you can install them by opening a command prompt, changing to the `twill-0.9` directory, and running:

```
$ python setup.py install
```

or, if you can't write to Python's `site-packages` directory,

```
$ python setup.py install --user
```

If you're using a version of Python older than 2.6, you won't be able to do a `--user` installation, which means you'll need to have write access to the Python installation's `site-packages` directory.

Exploring the Twill language

Now that you've installed Twill, you can open a shell program that lets you interactively explore its language and capabilities. We'll go through some of the most useful ones here.

Time for action – browsing the web with Twill

We'll take Twill for a spin, using its interactive interpreter.

1. Start the interactive Twill interpreter:

    ```
    $ twill-sh
    ```

    You may notice a couple of warnings about the deprecated md5 module when you start Twill. You may safely ignore them.

2. Get a list of Twill commands. You can get further information about a specific command by typing `help <command>` at the prompt.

`>> help`

```
-= Welcome to twill! =-

current page:  *empty page*
>> help

Undocumented commands:
======================
add_auth              fa           info            save_html        title
add_extra_header      find         load_cookies    setglobal        url
agent                 follow       notfind         setlocal
back                  formaction   redirect_error  show
clear_cookies         formclear    redirect_output show_cookies
clear_extra_headers   formfile     reload          show_extra_headers
code                  formvalue    reset_browser   showforms
config                fv           reset_error     showhistory
debug                 get_browser  reset_output    showlinks
echo                  getinput     run             sleep
exit                  getpassword  runfile         submit
extend_with           go           save_cookies    tidy_ok

current page:  *empty page*
>>
```

3. Tell Twill to go to a web site. Although `slashdot.org` is used in this example, the reader is encouraged to try out other sites as well.

`>> go http://slashdot.org/`

Twill will print out a couple of lines indicating that it is now browsing `http://slashdot.org/`.

4. Check that the web server returned a 'no error' code (which is to say, `code 200`). We could just as easily check for other codes—for example, making sure that our interface returned an error when asked to do something invalid.

`>> code 200`

5. Follow a link, which is specified by providing a regular expression. If you're not comfortable with regular expressions—or even if you are—you're usually fine by just specifying enough of the link text to identify the one that you want to follow. After following the link, check the code again to make sure it worked.

`>> follow Science`
`>> code 200`

6. Fill in a form field. This fills the first field of the second form with the word **monkey**. At the time of this writing, the second form is a search form, and the first field is the search box. If the page layout were to change, this example wouldn't be correct any more.

`>> formvalue 2 1 "monkey"`

7. We can also refer to forms and form fields by name (if they have names). The specific form used here doesn't have a name, but the field does. The following sets the value of the same field as the command in step 6, this time to the value **aardvark**.

```
>> formvalue 2 fhfilter "aardvark"
```

8. Now we can submit the form. This moves Twill to a new working URL, as well as sending information to the server.

```
>> submit
```

9. Once again, we want to make sure that the server returned the expected code.

```
>> code 200
```

10. Does the page contain what we expect? We can check with the `find` command. In this case, we'll be checking two things. The first is whether the word **aardvark** appears within the code of the result page. With the system currently in place on `slashdot.org`, we can expect that it will. The second check, for the word **Elephant** is probably going to fail.

```
>> find aardvark
```

```
>> find Elephant
```

```
>> find aardvark
current page: http://science.slashdot.org/index2.pl?fhfilter=aardvark
>> find Elephant

ERROR: no match to 'Elephant'

current page: http://science.slashdot.org/index2.pl?fhfilter=aardvark
>>
```

What just happened?

We used Twill to browse to `slashdot.org`, navigated into the **Science** section, searched for **aardvark**, and then checked to see if the resulting page contained the words **aardvark** and **Elephant**. Of what use it that?

We're not limited to goofing around on `slashdot.org`. We can use the Twill language to describe any interaction between a web browser and a web server. That means, we can use it to describe the expected behavior of our own web applications. If we can describe expected behavior, we can write tests.

It would be nice to be able to store the commands in a file though, so that we can automate the tests. Like any good interpreter, Twill will let us do that.

Time for action – Twill scripting

We'll write a Twill script that checks whether a site obeys the same interface that we used for interacting with slashdot.org, and then applies it to a few different web sites to see what happens.

1. Create a file called slashdot.twill containing the following code:

```
code 200
follow Science
code 200
formvalue 2 fhfilter "aardvark"
submit
code 200
find aardvark
```

2. Now, we'll run that script on http://slashdot.org/ and see whether it works.

```
$ twill-sh -u http://slashdot.org/ slashdot.twill
```

```
>> EXECUTING FILE slashdot.twill
==> at http://slashdot.org/
AT LINE: slashdot.twill:0
AT LINE: slashdot.twill:1
==> at http://science.slashdot.org
AT LINE: slashdot.twill:2
AT LINE: slashdot.twill:3
AT LINE: slashdot.twill:4
Note: submit is using submit button: name="None", value="Search"

AT LINE: slashdot.twill:5
AT LINE: slashdot.twill:6
--
1 of 1 files SUCCEEDED.
```

3. All right, that worked nicely. So, let's see if espn.com works the same way as slashdot.org did.

```
$ twill-sh -u http://espn.com/ slashdot.twill
```

```
>> EXECUTING FILE slashdot.twill
==> at http://espn.go.com/
AT LINE: slashdot.twill:0
AT LINE: slashdot.twill:1
Oops!  Twill assertion error on line 1 of 'slashdot.twill' while executing

  >> follow Science

no links match to 'Science'

** UNHANDLED EXCEPTION: no links match to 'Science'
--
0 of 1 files SUCCEEDED.
Failed:
        slashdot.twill
```

What just happened?

By storing the Twill commands in a file, we were able to run them as an automated test. That's definitely a step forward for testing our web-based applications.

The -u command line option that we passed to twill-sh is very useful: it has the same effect as a go command at the start of the file, but of course we can change it every time we run the script. This is particularly helpful if you're not sure what the base URL for your web app will end up being.

Twill commands

Twill has a number of commands, and so far we've only covered a few of them. In this section you'll find a brief discussion of each of Twill's commands.

help

The help command prints out a list of all of Twill's commands, or tells you the details of a specific command. For example, to get the details of the add_auth command, you should type:

```
>> help add_auth
```

```
>> help add_auth
===============

Help for command add_auth:

>> add_auth <realm> <uri> <user> <passwd>

    Add HTTP Basic Authentication information for the given realm/uri.

===============

current page:  *empty page*
>>
```

> If you want to know the detailed syntax of any of the other commands, use the help command to get that information.

setglobal

The setglobal command assigns a value to a variable name. These variable names can then be used as parameters of later commands. Thus, if you tell Twill to:

```
>> setglobal target http://www.example.org/
```

Twill will set the global variable target to the value `http://www.example.org/`. You would then be able to say:

```
>> go target
```

to tell Twill to go to `http://www.example.org/`.

Variable values can also be inserted into text strings by surrounding the variable name with `${` and `}`, so that:

```
>> go "${target}/example.html"
```

tells Twill to go to `http://www.example.org/example.html`.

setlocal

The `setlocal` command behaves generally like the `setglobal` command, with one significant difference; variables bound with `setlocal` only exist while Twill is executing the same script file (or, technically, interactive session) in which they were bound. Once Twill switches to a new script, local variables are forgotten until execution returns to the original script.

add_auth

The `add_auth` command lets you log in to a site protected by the Basic Authentication scheme of HTTP. The command takes four parameters, in this order: `realm`, `URI`, `username`, and `password`. The username and password are what a user would type in to gain access to the site. The URI is a prefix for all of the web addresses where you want the authentication to be applied: if you pass `http://example.com/` as the URI, the username and password might be used to login to any page on `example.com`. The realm is an arbitrary text string chosen by the server, which must be included in any authorization. If you're testing your own web app, you should already know what it is.

 You can find out all about HTTP Basic Authentication at `http://tools.ietf.org/html/rfc2617#section-2`.

So, to log in to the example realm on example.com with the username of `testuser` and the password of `12345`, you would use the following command:

```
>> add_auth example http://example.com/ testuser 12345
```

add_extra_header

By using `add_extra_header`, you can include any arbitrary HTTP header into all subsequent requests that Twill makes. The command takes two parameters: the name of the header field to be added, and the value to be assigned to the header field.

You need to keep in mind that HTTP allows the same header to exist multiple times in the same request, and to have different values each time. If you tell Twill

```
>> add_extra_header moose 12
>> add_extra_header moose 15
```

then there will be two 'moose' headers sent in each request, with different values.

clear_extra_headers

The `clear_extra_headers` command removes all of the previously defined extra headers from future requests. Removed headers can be re-added later.

show_extra_headers

The `show_extra_headers` command prints out a list of all of the currently added extra headers, along with their values.

agent

You can make Twill masquerade as a different web browser, by using the `agent` command. You can use any user agent string as the parameter. At the time of this writing, `http://user-agent-string.info/` was a useful resource for finding the user agent strings used by web browsers.

back

The `back` command works just as the back button on a web browser would, returning to the most recent URL in Twill's history.

clear_cookies

The `clear_cookies` command causes Twill to forget all of its currently stored cookies.

code

The `code` command checks that the HTTP response code from the previous navigation command was the expected value. The value that means 'success' is `200`. `404` means that the page wasn't found, `401` means that a login is required before you can browse the page, `301` and `302` are redirects, and so on.

 You can find a complete list of official HTTP response codes at `http://tools.ietf.org/html/rfc2616#section-6.1.1.`

config

The `config` command lets you modify the behavior of the Twill interpreter. It takes a configuration parameter name and an integer value as parameters, and Twill modifies its behavior according to the values given to the configuration variable.

For a complete list of current configuration variables, type:

```
>> help config
```

debug

The `debug` command causes Twill to output trace information as it operates. At the time of writing, there were three different kinds of debug trace available: HTTP, commands, and handling of the HTTP-EQUIV refresh tag.

If you tell Twill to:

```
>> debug http 1
```

then whenever Twill performs an HTTP operation, you'll see a printout of the request and response lines, along with the HTTP header fields that were returned with the response.

The `debug commands 1` command isn't useful when you're interacting directly with the Twill interpreter, but if you place it in a Twill script, it will cause Twill to print out each command as it executes, so that you can see what the script is doing.

If you tell Twill to

```
>> debug equiv-refresh 1
```

then it will print out extra information whenever it runs across a page with a `<META HTTP-EQUIV="refresh"...>` tag in the header.

echo

The `echo` command is useful if you want your Twill scripts to output information, but don't find that any of the `debug` subcommands really does what you want. Whatever parameters you pass to `echo`, are printed to the screen.

exit

The `exit` command causes the Twill interpreter to terminate. It takes an error code—which is just an integer, with 0 normally being interpreted as 'no error'—as an optional parameter. Even if you pass a non-zero value to `exit`, Twill will print out that the script succeeded, after all of the commands that it ran executed correctly, including `exit`. The error code is only meaningful if the program that executed Twill uses it, so in many cases it will be ignored completely.

extend_with

The `extend_with` command is a mechanism for customizing the Twill interpreter. It imports a Python module, and adds any functions in it as new Twill commands.

find

The `find` command searches the current page for text that matches a regular expression. Python's regular expression syntax is described in the online docs at `http://docs.python.org/library/re.html#regularexpressionsyntax`, but for our purposes it's enough to know that if you type a word, `find` will look for it.

The `find` command also accepts an optional second parameter. This parameter is a text string representing options controlling how the search is performed. If the string contains the letter `i` then the search is case-insensitive, meaning that capital and lowercase letters match with each other. The letters `m` and `s` mean to use 'MULTILINE' and 'DOTALL' modes, respectively. These modes are described in the above documentation.

The find command also binds the matched text to the local variable name __match__, so that you can refer to it in later commands, just as if it had been set by `setlocal`.

notfind

The `notfind` command works like the `find` command, except that if it finds a match for the regular expression, it fails. If it does not find a match, it succeeds.

follow

The `follow` command searches the current page for a link that matches a regular expression, and goes to the linked address. Using `follow` is like clicking on a link in a normal web browser.

Unlike the `find` command, the follow command does not accept regular expression flags, and does not bind the __match__ name. It just goes where the hyperlink points it.

formaction

The `formaction` command lets you change the address to which a form will be submitted. It takes two parameters: an identifier for the form you want to change, and the URL that you want the form submitted to.

For example, the following HTML would produce a form that would be submitted to the current URL, because that is the default when the `action` attribute is omitted from the `form` tag:

```
<form name="form1" method="post">
```

After executing this `formaction` command,

```
>> formaction form1 http://example.com/viewer
```

it would be as if the form had been written:

```
<form name="form1" method="post" action="http://example.com/viewer">
```

formclear

The `formclear` command resets a form to its initial state, meaning that data entered by other commands get forgotten.

formfile

The `formfile` command fills in a value for an `<input type="file">` form field. It has three required parameters: the form's name or number, the field's name or number, and the filename of the file. Optionally, a fourth parameter can be added which specifies the mime content type of the file.

formvalue

The `formvalue` command fills in values for HTML form fields. It accepts three parameters: the form's name or number, the field's name or number, and the value to be assigned. We used `formvalue` in the example Twill script above.

getinput

The `getinput` command allows Twill scripts to be interactive. The command accepts one parameter, a prompt that will be displayed to the user. After printing the prompt, Twill waits for the user to type something and hit enter, after which whatever the user typed is stored in the local variable called __input__.

getpassword

The `getpassword` command works mostly like `getinput`. The differences are that `getpassword` does not display the text that the user types, and that the text is bound to the local variable name __password__ after being input.

go

The go command directs Twill to go to a new URL and load the page at that address. Unlike follow, go doesn't care what links exist on the current page. Using go is like typing an address into the address bar of a normal web browser.

info

The info command prints some general information about the page that Twill is currently browsing. This information includes the URL, the HTTP code, the MIME content-type of the page, the title, and the number of forms on the page.

save_cookies

The save_cookies command saves a copy of any cookies that Twill is currently aware of. These cookies can be re-loaded later. The command takes a single parameter: the file name in which to store the cookies.

load_cookies

The load_cookies command replaces any cookies that Twill currently knows about with the cookies stored in a file. It takes a single parameter: the filename of the cookie file to load.

show_cookies

The show_cookies command will print out any cookies currently aware of.

redirect_error

The redirect_error command causes all of Twill's error messages to be stored in a file instead of being printed to the screen. It takes a single parameter representing the file name in which to store the errors.

redirect_output

The redirect_output command causes Twill to save all of its normal output to a file, instead of printing it to the screen. It takes a single parameter representing the file name in which to store the output.

This is not a command that will be of much use in an interactive Twill shell. It can be useful in scripts and tests.

reset_error

The reset_error command undoes the effect of redirect_error.

reset_output

The `reset_output` command undoes the effect of `redirect_output`.

reload

The `reload` command reloads the current URL, just as the reload or refresh button on a normal web browser would.

reset_browser

The `reset_browser` command destroys all of the state information pertaining to the current Twill session. It has the same effect as stopping Twill and then starting it up again.

run

The `run` command executes an arbitrary Python statement. The only parameter is the Python statement to execute. If the statement contains spaces, it must be placed within quotes, so Twill doesn't mistake it for multiple parameters.

runfile

The runfile command executes a Twill script that's stored in a separate file. The executed script will have its own local namespace (c.f. the `setlocal` command), and will share the global namespace (c.f. `setglobal`)

save_html

The `save_html` command saves the HTML content of the current page into a file. It accepts a filename to save into as an optional parameter. If no filename is specified, Twill will choose for itself based on the URL of the data being saved.

show

The `show` command prints out the HTML content of the current page. This can be useful in an interactive session for getting a handle on what Twill is seeing, and it can occasionally be useful in a test script if you want to make sure that a page has precisely specified content.

showforms

The `showforms` command prints out a list of all of the forms in the current page. Each form has a printout containing the form's number (and name, if it has a name), along with the numbers, names, types, ids, and current values for each field.

showhistory

The showhistory command prints out a list of all of the URLs previously visited in the current Twill session, in order from oldest to most recent.

showlinks

The showlinks command prints out a (potentially quite long) list of the links in the current page. This can be helpful for figuring out what you need to type into the follow command, or just for general debugging.

sleep

The sleep command can be used to inject pauses in the execution of a Twill script. It accepts one optional parameter specifying the number of seconds to pause before continuing to execute the script. If the time is not specified, it defaults to one second.

submit

The submit command submits the form containing the field most recently changed by the formvalue command. It accepts one optional parameter specifying which submit button to use, specified in the same way a field would be specified for the formvalue command. If the submit button is not specified, the first one in the form is used.

tidy_ok

If you have HTML Tidy (http://tidy.sourceforge.net/) installed, the tidy_ok command will use it to check whether the current page's code is correct. If you put tidy_ok in a script and the current page does not meet Tidy's standards of correctness, the script will be considered a failure.

title

The title command accepts a regular expression as its only parameter, and tries to match the current page's title against the regular expression. If they don't match, the title command fails. Used in a script file, this will cause the entire script to be considered a failure if the title does not match.

url

The url command accepts a regular expression as it's only parameter, and tries to match the current page's URL against the regular expression. If they don't match, the url command fails, and causes the script it's part of to fail. If the regular expression does match the URL, the local variable __match__ is bound to the matching part of the URL.

Pop quiz – the Twill language

1. Which form is submitted when you use the `submit` command?
2. Which command would you use to check that an error message is not on the page?
3. When you're executing a Twill script and a command fails, what happens?

Have a go hero – browsing the web with Twill

Open up a Twill interactive shell, use it to search Google, follow one of the links in the search result, and navigate around the linked site. While you're doing that, try to get some hands on experience with as many of the Twill commands as you can.

Calling Twill scripts from tests

While it's nice to be able to use `twill-sh` to execute a bunch of Twill scripts as a form of automated testing, we'd really like to be able to run the Twill scripts as part of our normal test suite. Fortunately, it's fairly easy to do so. There are two nice ways to run Twill scripts from Python code, and you can choose whichever better suits your needs.

Time for action – running Twill script files

The first way is to store the Twill script in a separate file, and then use the `twill.parse.execute_file` function to run it.

1. Place the following code into a file called `fail.twill`:

   ```
   go http://slashdot.org/
   find this_does_not_exist
   ```

2. Naturally, this script will fail, but go ahead and run it with `twill-sh` to see for yourself.

   ```
   $ twill-sh fail.twill
   ```

3. Now to run the script from Python. Pull up an interactive Python shell and do the following:

```
>>> from twill.parse import execute_file
>>> execute_file('fail.twill')
```

```
AT LINE: fail.twill:0
==> at http://slashdot.org/
AT LINE: fail.twill:1
Oops! Twill assertion error on line 1 of 'fail.twill' while executing

>> find this_does_not_exist

no match to 'this_does_not_exist'

Traceback (most recent call last):
  File "<stdin>", line 1, in <module>
  File "/home/djarb/local/lib/python2.6/site-packages/twill-0.9-py2.6.egg/twill/parse.py", line 179, in execute_file
    _execute_script(inp, **kw)
  File "/home/djarb/local/lib/python2.6/site-packages/twill-0.9-py2.6.egg/twill/parse.py", line 222, in _execute_script
    execute_command(cmd, args, globals_dict, locals_dict, cmdinfo)
  File "/home/djarb/local/lib/python2.6/site-packages/twill-0.9-py2.6.egg/twill/parse.py", line 127, in execute_command
    result = eval(codeobj, globals_dict, locals_dict)
  File "fail.twill:1", line 1, in <module>
  File "/home/djarb/local/lib/python2.6/site-packages/twill-0.9-py2.6.egg/twill/commands.py", line 239, in find
    raise TwillAssertionError("no match to '%s'" % (what,))
twill.errors.TwillAssertionError: no match to 'this_does_not_exist'
>>>
```

4. Simple as that, we ran the script from inside Python code. That would work equally well in doctest, unittest, or in nose-specific test code.

5. Notice that what the Twill shell would report as an error, execute_file reports as a `twill.errors.TwillAssertionError` exception. That integrates nicely with the automated testing tools we've discussed previously.

What just happened?

With just a couple of lines of code, we executed a Twill script that was stored in a separate file, and received any errors that it encountered as Python exceptions. This is ideal for situations where you have a pre-existing Twill script, and just want a way to have it run alongside the rest of your test suite. It's also convenient if you want to automatically generate the Twill script, or if you simply want to keep different languages in different files.

Time for action – running Twill script strings

The second way to run a Twill script from inside Python code is to store the script in a string.

1. Open up an interactive Python interpreter and type the following commands:

```
>>> from twill.parse import execute_string
>>> execute_string("""
... go http://slashdot.org/
... find this_does_not_exist
... """, no_reset = False)
```

2. The result will be just the same as when we executed a file containing those commands.

 Notice the `no_reset = False` parameter that we passed to `execute_string`. We need that because if we leave it out, Twill will assume that all of our calls to `execute_string` should be executed, as if they were all part of the same browser session. We don't want that because we want our tests to be separated from each other. `execute_file` will make the opposite assumption, so, we don't need to pass it a `no_reset` parameter (although we could).

What just happened?

This time, the script was embedded directly into the Python code as a string constant. This is desirable when the Twill script is seen as simply being another way to write part of a test, rather than a separate thing in itself.

A nifty trick

If you're using Python 2.4 or greater, you can define a function decorator that makes it simple to write Twill tests as Python functions.

```
from twill.parse import execute_string
from twill.errors import TwillAssertionError
def twill_test(func):
    def run_test(*args):
        try:
            execute_string(func.__doc__, no_reset = False)
        except TwillAssertionError, err:
            if args and hasattr(args[0], 'fail'):
                args[0].fail(str(err))
            else:
                raise
    return run_test
```

If you put that code in a Python module (here called `twill_decorator`) and then import `twill_test` into your testing code, you can write Twill tests like so:

```
from unittest import TestCase
from twill_decorator import twill_test
class web_tests(TestCase):
    @twill_test
    def test_slashdot(self):
        """
        go http://slashdot.org/
        find this_does_not_exist
        """
```

When you use Nose or unittest to run that test module, the `test_slashdot` function will automatically execute the Twill script in its document string, and report any errors as test failures. You don't have to remember to pass `no_reset = False`, or any of the other details of running Twill from a string.

Integrating Twill operations into unittest tests

So far, our unit tests have treated each Twill script as a single operation that produces either a success or a failure. What if we want to, say, download an HTML page, perform some assertions about relationships between its content and a database, then follow a link to another page?

We can do this sort of thing by accessing Twill's browser object directly from our test code. The browser object has methods similar to the commands of the Twill language, so this should seem fairly familiar.

Time for action – using Twill's browser object

Here we see how to access the browser object directly, and use it to interact with the web.

1. Place the following code into a Python test module:

```
from unittest import TestCase
import twill

class test_twill_browser(TestCase):
    def test_slashdot(self):
        browser = twill.get_browser()

        browser.go('http://slashdot.org/')
        self.assertTrue(browser.get_code() in (200, 201))

        html = browser.get_html()
        self.assertTrue(html.count('slashdot') > 150)

        link = browser.find_link('Science')
        browser.follow_link(link)

        form = browser.get_form(2)
        form.set_value('aardvark', name = 'fhfilter')
        browser.clicked(form, None)
        browser.submit()
        self.assertEqual(browser.get_code(), 200)
```

2. Run the test module using `nosetests`. If Slashdot hasn't changed their interface since this was written, then the test will pass. If they have, the test will probably fail.

What just happened?

Instead of using the Twill language to describe the interaction with a web site, we used Twill as a library that we could call from our test code. This allowed us to interleave Twill operations with unittest assertions. We could have included any other operations that we needed, as well. Using this technique, our tests can treat the web as just one more source of data that they can access.

It's important to notice the differences between the Twill language and the methods available on the browser object. For example, where the Twill language has a show command that prints out the HTML of the current page, the browser has a get_html method that returns the HTML of the current page.

Pay special attention to the interactions with the form, at the end of the test. These interactions use a form object, which can be retrieved by calling the browser object's get_form method.

The set_value method of a form object accepts the new value for the control as the first parameter, and then has a number of keyword arguments that can be used to specify which control should take on that value. The most useful of these arguments are name, as used above, and nr, which selects the control by number.

In order for submit to work, it should be preceded by a call to the clicked method targeting one of the controls of the form (it doesn't matter which).

Browser methods

The browser object retrieved with twill.get_browser() has the following useful methods:

- go
- reload
- back
- get_code
- get_html
- get_title
- get_url
- find_link
- follow_link
- set_agent_string
- get_all_forms
- get_form

- get_form_field
- clicked
- submit
- save_cookies
- load_cookies
- clear_cookies

Many of those work just as the related Twill command, except that you pass the parameters as strings into a method call [e.g. browser.save_cookies('cookies.txt')]. A few of them behave differently, though, or don't have a Twill language equivalent, so we'll go into more detail about those now:

get_code

The get_code method returns the HTTP code for the current page. It doesn't do any comparisons between the code and an expected value. If you want to raise an exception if the code isn't 200, you need to do it yourself.

get_html

The get_html method returns the HTML for the current page as a Python string.

get_title

The get_title method returns the title of the current page as a Python string.

get_url

The get_url method returns the URL of the current page as a Python string.

find_link

The find_link method searches for a link whose URL, text or name matches matches the regular expression that was passed in as a parameter. If it finds such a link, it returns an object representing that link. If no such link exists, find_link returns None.

A link object has a number of useful attributes. If you have a link object named link, then link.attrs is a list of (name, value) tuples, link.text is the text appearing between the <a> and </a> tags, and link.absolute_url is the address to which the link points.

follow_link

The `follow_link` method takes a link object as a parameter, and goes to the address represented by the link. If you have a URL in the form of a string, rather than a link object, you should use the `go` method instead.

get_all_forms

The `get_all_forms` method returns a list of form objects representing all forms appearing in the page. If there are any form controls on the page that aren't inside of `<form>` tags, a special form object will be created to contain them, and will be the first element of the list.

get_form

The `get_form` method takes a regular expression as a parameter, and searches for a form whose id, name or number matches. If it finds such a form, it returns a form object representing it.

A form object has several useful attributes. If you have a form object called `form`, then `form.name` is the name of the form if it has a name, `form.method` is the form's method (usually 'GET' or 'POST'), `form.action` is the URL to which the form should be submitted, `form.enctype` is the content type to use when encoding the form for transmission, and `form.attrs` is a dictionary of attributes applied to the form.

A form object also has methods that help you manipulate its contents. Notable among these are `form.get_value`, `form.set_value`, `form.clear`, `form.clear_all`, and `form.add_file`. All of these methods except for `clear_all` target a specific control within the form. You tell it which control to target by passing one or more of the following keyword arguments to the method: `name`, `type`, `kind`, `id`, `nr`, and `label`. The `nr` keyword is short for 'number'. If no control matches all of the specified parameters, an `_mechanize_dist.ClientForm.ControlNotFoundError` exception will be raised.

The `set_value` and `add_file` methods accept a value or a filename, respectively, as their first parameters. The `get_value` method returns the current value of the selected control. The `clear` method returns a control to its default value.

get_form_field

The `get_form_field` method takes a form object as its first parameter and a regular expression as its second. If precisely one of the form's controls has an id, name or index that matches the regular expression, an object representing that control is returned.

For the most part this is not needed, because the form object's methods are more flexible ways to manipulate form controls. Its primary use is to provide input to the `clicked` method.

clicked

The `clicked` method exists to keep the browser object appraised about which part of the page is the current focus. In particular, this tells it which form to submit when the `submit` method is called.

The `clicked` method takes two parameters: the form object that will become the focus, and the specific control within the form where the click should be registered.

It is usually simplest to pass `None` as the specific control. You may, however, pass a control object (as returned by `get_form_field`). If this control object represents a submit control, that control becomes the new default to use when submitting the form. The initial default is the first submit control in the form.

submit

The `submit` method submits the last-clicked form, as per its `action` and `method`. You may optionally pass a `fieldname` parameter representing which submit control to use for the submission. If it exists, this parameter will be passed to `get_form_field` to find the appropriate submit control. If you don't pass a `fieldname` to the method, the default submit control will be used.

Pop quiz – browser methods

1. How do you indicate which form object you want to retrieve when you call `get_form`?
2. What does the `clicked` method do?
3. How does the `get_code` method differ from the `code` command?

Summary

We learned a lot in this chapter about Twill, and how to use it to write tests for web applications.

Specifically, we covered:

- The Twill language
- Invoking Twill scripts from Python tests
- Integrating Twill's capabilities as a library into Python testing code

Now that we've learned about testing web applications, we're ready to move on to talking about integration testing and system testing – which is the topic of the next chapter.

9

Integration Testing and System Testing

With all of the tools, techniques, and practices that we've discussed so far, we've still only been been thinking about testing units: the smallest meaningfully testable pieces of code. It's time to expand the focus and start testing code that incorporates multiple units.

In this chapter, we shall:

- ◆ Describe integration testing and system testing
- ◆ Learn how to break up a program into testable multi-unit sections
- ◆ Use doctest, unittest, and Nose to automate multi-unit tests

So let's get on with it!

Integration tests and system tests

Integration testing is the process of checking that the units making up your program work correctly in concert with each other, rather than in isolation. It's not practical to start the process with integration testing, because if the units don't work, the integration won't work either, and it will be harder to track down the cause of your problems. Once your units are solid though, it's necessary to test that the things you build out of them also work. The interactions between units can be surprising.

While you perform integration testing, you'll be putting the units together into bigger and bigger collections and testing those collections. When your integration tests expand to cover the entirety of your program, they have become system tests.

The trickiest part of integration testing is choosing which units to integrate into each test, so that you always have a solid base of code that you can believe in; a place to stand, while you pull in more code.

Time for action – figuring out the order of integration

We'll walk through an exercise that can help with the process of deciding where to put the boundaries of integration tests.

1. Using a piece of paper or a graphics program, write out names or representations for each of the units in the time planner project from Chapter 7. Group the methods of each class together. Being part of the same class is an obvious relationship between units, and we'll take advantage of that. (The == symbol here represents the Python == operator, which invokes the __eq__ method on an object).

activities	statuses	schedules	file
excludes	excludes	add	store_object
overlaps	overlaps	remove	load_object
==	==	store	
		load	
		in	
		==	

2. Now, draw arrows between units that are supposed to directly interact with each other, from the caller to the callee. Laying everything out in an orderly fashion (like in step 1) can actually make this harder, so feel free to move the classes around to help the lines make sense.

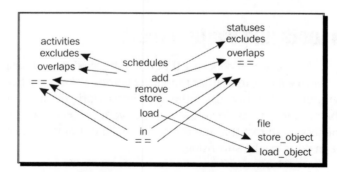

3. Draw circles around each class and each pair of classes that is connected by at least one line.

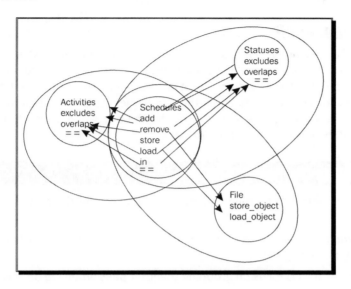

4. Continue the process by drawing circles around overlapping pairs of circles, until there are only three circles left. Circle a pair of them and then put one more big circle around the whole mess.

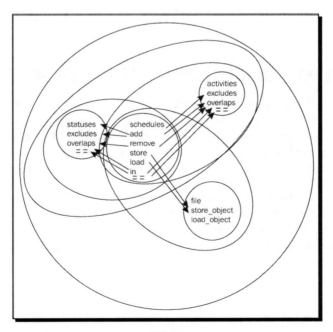

5. These circles tell us which order to write our integration tests in. The smaller the circle, the sooner the test should be written.

What just happened?

What we just did is a way to visualize and concretize the process of building up integration tests. While it's not critical to actually draw the lines and circles, it's useful to follow the process in your head. For larger projects, a lot can be gained from actually drawing the diagrams. When you can see the diagram, the correct next step tends to jump right out at you—especially if you use multiple colors to render the diagram—where it might otherwise be hidden behind the complexity of the program.

Pop quiz – diagramming integration

1. What's the point of grouping units together into classes during the early part of this process?

2. When we move classes around to help the arrows make sense, what effect does that have on the later process?

3. Why do we always focus on grouping together pairs when we do this?

Have a go hero – diagram your own program

Take one of your own programs and build an integration diagram for it. If your program is large enough that the diagram begins to get clumsy, try putting different 'levels' of the diagram on separate pages.

Automation with doctest, unittest, and Nose

The only real difference between an integration test and a unit test, is that you could break the code being tested into smaller meaningful chunks, in an integration test. In a unit test, if you divided the code up any more it wouldn't be meaningful. For this reason, the same tools that help automate unit testing can be applied to integration testing. Since system testing is really the highest level of integration testing, the tools can be used for that as well.

The role of doctest in integration testing tends to be fairly limited. The real strengths of doctest are in the early part of the development process. It's easy for a testable specification to stray into integration testing—as mentioned before, that's fine as long as there are unit tests as well—but after that it's likely that you'll prefer unittest and Nose for writing your integration tests.

Integration tests need to be isolated from each other. Even though they contain multiple interacting units within themselves, you still benefit from knowing that nothing outside the test is affecting it. For this reason, unittest is a good choice for writing automated integration tests. Working together with unittest, Nose and Mocker complete the picture nicely.

Time for action – writing integration tests for the time planner

Now that we've got an integration diagram for the time planner code, we can move ahead with actually writing automated integration tests.

1. The integration diagram provides only a partial ordering of the integration tests, and there are several tests that could be the first one we write. Looking at the diagram, we see that the `statuses` and `activities` classes are at the ends of a lot of arrows, but not at the beginnings of any. This makes them particularly good places to start, because it means that they don't call on anything outside of themselves to operate. Since there's nothing to distinguish one of them as a better place to start than the other, we can choose between them arbitrarily. Let's start with `statuses`, and then do `activities`. We're going to write tests that exercise the whole class. At this low level, the integration tests will look a lot like the unit tests for the same class, but we're not going to use mock objects to represent other instances of the same class: we'll use real instances. We're testing whether the class correctly interacts with itself.

2. Here is the test code for `statuses`:

```python
from unittest import TestCase
from planner.data import statuses, task_error
from datetime import datetime

class statuses_integration_tests(TestCase):
    def setUp(self):
        self.A = statuses('A',
                          datetime(year=2008, month=7, day=15),
                          datetime(year=2009, month=5, day=2))

    def test_repr(self):
        self.assertEqual(repr(self.A), '<A 2008-07-15T00:00:00
2009-05-02T00:00:00>')

    def test_equality(self):
        self.assertEqual(self.A, self.A)
        self.assertNotEqual(self.A, statuses('B',
                          datetime(year=2008, month=7, day=15),
                          datetime(year=2009, month=5, day=2)))
        self.assertNotEqual(self.A, statuses('A',
                          datetime(year=2007, month=7, day=15),
```

```
                                    datetime(year=2009, month=5, day=2)))
        self.assertNotEqual(self.A, statuses('A',
                        datetime(year=2008, month=7, day=15),
                        datetime(year=2010, month=5, day=2)))

    def test_overlap_begin(self):
        status = statuses('status name',
                        datetime(year=2007, month=8, day=11),
                        datetime(year=2008, month=11, day=27))

        self.assertTrue(status.overlaps(self.A))

    def test_overlap_end(self):
        status = statuses('status name',
                        datetime(year=2008, month=1, day=11),
                        datetime(year=2010, month=4, day=16))

        self.assertTrue(status.overlaps(self.A))

    def test_overlap_inner(self):
        status = statuses('status name',
                        datetime(year=2007, month=10, day=11),
                        datetime(year=2010, month=1, day=27))

        self.assertTrue(status.overlaps(self.A))

    def test_overlap_outer(self):
        status = statuses('status name',
                        datetime(year=2008, month=8, day=12),
                        datetime(year=2008, month=9, day=15))

        self.assertTrue(status.overlaps(self.A))

    def test_overlap_after(self):
        status = statuses('status name',
                        datetime(year=2011, month=2, day=6),
                        datetime(year=2015, month=4, day=27))

        self.assertFalse(status.overlaps(self.A))
```

3. Here is the test code for `activities`:

```
from unittest import TestCase
from planner.data import activities, task_error
from datetime import datetime

class activities_integration_tests(TestCase):
    def setUp(self):
        self.A = activities('A',
                        datetime(year=2008, month=7, day=15),
                        datetime(year=2009, month=5, day=2))

    def test_repr(self):
        self.assertEqual(repr(self.A), '<A 2008-07-15T00:00:00
2009-05-02T00:00:00>')

    def test_equality(self):
```

```
        self.assertEqual(self.A, self.A)
        self.assertNotEqual(self.A, activities('B',
                            datetime(year=2008, month=7, day=15),
                            datetime(year=2009, month=5, day=2)))
        self.assertNotEqual(self.A, activities('A',
                            datetime(year=2007, month=7, day=15),
                            datetime(year=2009, month=5, day=2)))
        self.assertNotEqual(self.A, activities('A',
                            datetime(year=2008, month=7, day=15),
                            datetime(year=2010, month=5, day=2)))

    def test_overlap_begin(self):
        activity = activities('activity name',
                            datetime(year=2007, month=8, day=11),
                            datetime(year=2008, month=11, day=27))

        self.assertTrue(activity.overlaps(self.A))
        self.assertTrue(activity.excludes(self.A))

    def test_overlap_end(self):
        activity = activities('activity name',
                            datetime(year=2008, month=1, day=11),
                            datetime(year=2010, month=4, day=16))

        self.assertTrue(activity.overlaps(self.A))
        self.assertTrue(activity.excludes(self.A))

    def test_overlap_inner(self):
        activity = activities('activity name',
                            datetime(year=2007, month=10, day=11),
                            datetime(year=2010, month=1, day=27))

        self.assertTrue(activity.overlaps(self.A))
        self.assertTrue(activity.excludes(self.A))

    def test_overlap_outer(self):
        activity = activities('activity name',
                            datetime(year=2008, month=8, day=12),
                            datetime(year=2008, month=9, day=15))

        self.assertTrue(activity.overlaps(self.A))
        self.assertTrue(activity.excludes(self.A))

    def test_overlap_after(self):
        activity = activities('activity name',
                            datetime(year=2011, month=2, day=6),
                            datetime(year=2015, month=4, day=27))

        self.assertFalse(activity.overlaps(self.A))
```

4. Looking at our diagram, we can see that the next level out from either `statuses` or `activities` represents the integration of those classes with the `schedules` class. Before we write that integration, we ought to write any tests that involve the schedules class interacting with itself, without mocking it.

```
from unittest import TestCase
from mocker import MockerTestCase, MATCH, ANY
from planner.data import schedules, schedule_error
from datetime import datetime

class schedules_tests(MockerTestCase):
    def setUp(self):
        mocker = self.mocker

        A = mocker.mock()
        A.__eq__(MATCH(lambda x: x is A))
        mocker.result(True)
        mocker.count(0, None)
        A.__eq__(MATCH(lambda x: x is not A))
        mocker.result(False)
        mocker.count(0, None)
        A.overlaps(ANY)
        mocker.result(False)
        mocker.count(0, None)
        A.begins
        mocker.result(5)
        mocker.count(0, None)

        B = mocker.mock()
        A.__eq__(MATCH(lambda x: x is B))
        mocker.result(True)
        mocker.count(0, None)
        B.__eq__(MATCH(lambda x: x is not B))
        mocker.result(False)
        mocker.count(0, None)
        B.overlaps(ANY)
        mocker.result(False)
        mocker.count(0, None)
        B.begins
        mocker.result(3)
        mocker.count(0, None)

        C = mocker.mock()
        C.__eq__(MATCH(lambda x: x is C))
        mocker.result(True)
        mocker.count(0, None)
        C.__eq__(MATCH(lambda x: x is not C))
        mocker.result(False)
        mocker.count(0, None)
        C.overlaps(ANY)
```

```
        mocker.result(False)
        mocker.count(0, None)
        C.begins
        mocker.result(7)
        mocker.count(0, None)

        self.A = A
        self.B = B
        self.C = C

        mocker.replay()
    def test_equality(self):
        sched1 = schedules()
        sched2 = schedules()

        self.assertEqual(sched1, sched2)

        sched1.add(self.A)
        sched1.add(self.B)

        sched2.add(self.A)
        sched2.add(self.B)
        sched2.add(self.C)

        self.assertNotEqual(sched1, sched2)

        sched1.add(self.C)

        self.assertEqual(sched1, sched2)
```

5. Now that interactions within the `schedules` class have been tested, we can write tests that integrate `schedules` and one of `statuses` or `activities`. Let's start with `statuses`, then do `activities`. Here are the tests for `schedules` and `statuses`:

```
from planner.data import schedules, statuses
from unittest import TestCase
from datetime import datetime, timedelta

class test_schedules_and_statuses(TestCase):
    def setUp(self):
        self.A = statuses('A',
                          datetime.now(),
                          datetime.now() + timedelta(minutes = 7))
        self.B = statuses('B',
                          datetime.now() - timedelta(hours = 1),
                          datetime.now() + timedelta(hours = 1))
        self.C = statuses('C',
                          datetime.now() + timedelta(minutes = 10),
                          datetime.now() + timedelta(hours = 1))
    def test_usage_pattern(self):
        sched = schedules()
```

```
        sched.add(self.A)
        sched.add(self.C)

        self.assertTrue(self.A in sched)
        self.assertTrue(self.C in sched)
        self.assertFalse(self.B in sched)

        sched.add(self.B)

        self.assertTrue(self.B in sched)

        self.assertEqual(sched, sched)

        sched.remove(self.A)

        self.assertFalse(self.A in sched)
        self.assertTrue(self.B in sched)
        self.assertTrue(self.C in sched)

        sched.remove(self.B)
        sched.remove(self.C)

        self.assertFalse(self.B in sched)
        self.assertFalse(self.C in sched)
```

6. Here are the tests for `schedules` and `activities`:

```
from planner.data import schedules, activities, schedule_error
from unittest import TestCase
from datetime import datetime, timedelta

class test_schedules_and_activities(TestCase):
    def setUp(self):
        self.A = activities('A',
                            datetime.now(),
                            datetime.now() + timedelta(minutes = 7))
        self.B = activities('B',
                            datetime.now() - timedelta(hours = 1),
                            datetime.now() + timedelta(hours = 1))
        self.C = activities('C',
                            datetime.now() + timedelta(minutes =
                                                        10),
                            datetime.now() + timedelta(hours = 1))

    def test_usage_pattern(self):
        sched = schedules()

        sched.add(self.A)
        sched.add(self.C)

        self.assertTrue(self.A in sched)
        self.assertTrue(self.C in sched)
        self.assertFalse(self.B in sched)

        self.assertRaises(schedule_error, sched.add, self.B)

        self.assertFalse(self.B in sched)
```

```
        self.assertEqual(sched, sched)

        sched.remove(self.A)

        self.assertFalse(self.A in sched)
        self.assertFalse(self.B in sched)
        self.assertTrue(self.C in sched)

        sched.remove(self.C)

        self.assertFalse(self.B in sched)
        self.assertFalse(self.C in sched)
```

7. It's time to pull `schedules`, `statuses`, and `activities` all together into the same tests.

```
from planner.data import schedules, statuses, activities,
schedule_error
from unittest import TestCase
from datetime import datetime, timedelta

class test_schedules_activities_and_statuses(TestCase):
    def setUp(self):
        self.A = statuses('A',
                          datetime.now(),
                          datetime.now() + timedelta(minutes = 7))
        self.B = statuses('B',
                          datetime.now() - timedelta(hours = 1),
                          datetime.now() + timedelta(hours = 1))
        self.C = statuses('C',
                          datetime.now() + timedelta(minutes = 10),
                          datetime.now() + timedelta(hours = 1))

        self.D = activities('D',
                            datetime.now(),
                            datetime.now() + timedelta(minutes = 7))

        self.E = activities('E',
                            datetime.now() + timedelta(minutes=30),
                            datetime.now() + timedelta(hours=1))

        self.F = activities('F',
                            datetime.now() - timedelta(minutes=20),
                            datetime.now() + timedelta(minutes=40))

    def test_usage_pattern(self):
        sched = schedules()

        sched.add(self.A)
        sched.add(self.B)
        sched.add(self.C)

        sched.add(self.D)

        self.assertTrue(self.A in sched)
        self.assertTrue(self.B in sched)
```

```
        self.assertTrue(self.C in sched)
        self.assertTrue(self.D in sched)

        self.assertRaises(schedule_error, sched.add, self.F)
        self.assertFalse(self.F in sched)

        sched.add(self.E)
        sched.remove(self.D)

        self.assertTrue(self.E in sched)
        self.assertFalse(self.D in sched)

        self.assertRaises(schedule_error, sched.add, self.F)

        self.assertFalse(self.F in sched)

        sched.remove(self.E)

        self.assertFalse(self.E in sched)

        sched.add(self.F)

        self.assertTrue(self.F in sched)
```

8. The next thing that we need to pull in is the `file` class, but before we integrate it with the rest of the system, we need to integrate it with itself; checking its internal interactions without using mock objects.

```
from unittest import TestCase
from planner.persistence import file
from os import unlink

class test_file(TestCase):
    def setUp(self):
        storage = file('file_test.sqlite')

        storage.store_object('tag1', 'A')
        storage.store_object('tag2', 'B')
        storage.store_object('tag1', 'C')
        storage.store_object('tag1', 'D')
        storage.store_object('tag3', 'E')
        storage.store_object('tag3', 'F')

    def tearDown(self):
        unlink('file_test.sqlite')

    def test_other_instance(self):
        storage = file('file_test.sqlite')

        self.assertEqual(set(storage.load_objects('tag1')),
                    set(['A', 'C', 'D']))

        self.assertEqual(set(storage.load_objects('tag2')),
                    set(['B']))

        self.assertEqual(set(storage.load_objects('tag3')),
                    set(['E', 'F']))
```

9. Now we can write tests that integrate `schedules` and `file`. Notice that for this step, we still aren't involving `statuses` or `activities`, because they're outside the oval.

```
from mocker import Mocker, MockerTestCase, ANY
from planner.data import schedules
from planner.persistence import file
from os import unlink

def unpickle_mocked_task(begins):
    mocker = Mocker()
    ret = mocker.mock()
    ret.overlaps(ANY)
    mocker.result(False)
    mocker.count(0, None)
    ret.begins
    mocker.result(begins)
    mocker.count(0, None)
    mocker.replay()
    return ret
unpickle_mocked_task.__safe_for_unpickling__ = True

class test_schedules_and_file(MockerTestCase):
    def setUp(self):
        mocker = self.mocker

        A = mocker.mock()
        A.overlaps(ANY)
        mocker.result(False)
        mocker.count(0, None)
        A.begins
        mocker.result(5)
        mocker.count(0, None)
        A.__reduce_ex__(ANY)
        mocker.result((unpickle_mocked_task, (5,)))
        mocker.count(0, None)

        B = mocker.mock()
        B.overlaps(ANY)
        mocker.result(False)
        mocker.count(0, None)
        B.begins
        mocker.result(3)
        mocker.count(0, None)
        B.__reduce_ex__(ANY)
        mocker.result((unpickle_mocked_task, (3,)))
        mocker.count(0, None)

        C = mocker.mock()
        C.overlaps(ANY)
        mocker.result(False)
```

```
                   mocker.count(0, None)
                   C.begins
                   mocker.result(7)
                   mocker.count(0, None)
                   C.__reduce_ex__(ANY)
                   mocker.result((unpickle_mocked_task, (7,)))
                   mocker.count(0, None)

                   self.A = A
                   self.B = B
                   self.C = C

                   mocker.replay()
           def tearDown(self):
               try:
                   unlink('test_schedules_and_file.sqlite')
               except OSError:
                   pass
           def test_save_and_restore(self):
               sched1 = schedules()

               sched1.add(self.A)
               sched1.add(self.B)
               sched1.add(self.C)

               store1 = file('test_schedules_and_file.sqlite')
               sched1.store(store1)

               del sched1
               del store1

               store2 = file('test_schedules_and_file.sqlite')
               sched2 = schedules.load(store2)

               self.assertEqual(set([x.begins for x in sched2.tasks]),
                                set([3, 5, 7]))
```

10. We've built our way up to the outermost circle now, which means that it's time to write tests that involve the whole system, with no mock objects anywhere.

```
from planner.data import schedules, statuses, activities,
schedule_error
from planner.persistence import file
from unittest import TestCase
from datetime import datetime, timedelta
from os import unlink

class test_system(TestCase):
    def setUp(self):
        self.A = statuses('A',
                          datetime.now(),
                          datetime.now() + timedelta(minutes = 7))
```

```
            self.B = statuses('B',
                              datetime.now() - timedelta(hours = 1),
                              datetime.now() + timedelta(hours = 1))
            self.C = statuses('C',
                              datetime.now() + timedelta(minutes = 10),
                              datetime.now() + timedelta(hours = 1))
            self.D = activities('D',
                                datetime.now(),
                                datetime.now() + timedelta(minutes = 7))
            self.E = activities('E',
                                datetime.now() + timedelta(minutes=30),
                                datetime.now() + timedelta(hours = 1))
            self.F = activities('F',
                                datetime.now() - timedelta(minutes=20),
                                datetime.now() + timedelta(minutes=40))
        def tearDown(self):
            try:
                unlink('test_system.sqlite')
            except OSError:
                pass
        def test_usage_pattern(self):
            sched1 = schedules()
            sched1.add(self.A)
            sched1.add(self.B)
            sched1.add(self.C)
            sched1.add(self.D)
            sched1.add(self.E)
            store1 = file('test_system.sqlite')
            sched1.store(store1)
            del store1
            store2 = file('test_system.sqlite')
            sched2 = schedules.load(store2)
            self.assertEqual(sched1, sched2)
            sched2.remove(self.D)
            sched2.remove(self.E)
            self.assertNotEqual(sched1, sched2)
            sched2.add(self.F)
            self.assertTrue(self.F in sched2)
            self.assertFalse(self.F in sched1)
            self.assertRaises(schedule_error, sched2.add, self.D)
            self.assertRaises(schedule_error, sched2.add, self.E)
            self.assertTrue(self.A in sched1)
```

```
        self.assertTrue(self.B in sched1)
        self.assertTrue(self.C in sched1)
        self.assertTrue(self.D in sched1)
        self.assertTrue(self.E in sched1)
        self.assertFalse(self.F in sched1)

        self.assertTrue(self.A in sched2)
        self.assertTrue(self.B in sched2)
        self.assertTrue(self.C in sched2)
        self.assertFalse(self.D in sched2)
        self.assertFalse(self.E in sched2)
        self.assertTrue(self.F in sched2)
```

What just happened?

We've just tested our whole code base, always being careful to test one thing at a time. Because we took care to go step-by-step, we always knew where newly discovered bugs originated, and we were able to fix them easily.

Let's take a moment to examine each section of the code.

```
class statuses_integration_tests(TestCase):
    def setUp(self):
        self.A = statuses('A',
                          datetime(year=2008, month=7, day=15),
                          datetime(year=2009, month=5, day=2))
```

We're creating a status object here in our `setUp` method. Because it's a `setUp` method—part of the test fixture—each test will have its own unique version of `self.A`, and changes made in one test won't be visible to any other test.

```
    def test_equality(self):
        self.assertEqual(self.A, self.A)
        self.assertNotEqual(self.A, statuses('B',
                          datetime(year=2008, month=7, day=15),
                          datetime(year=2009, month=5, day=2)))
        self.assertNotEqual(self.A, statuses('A',
                          datetime(year=2007, month=7, day=15),
                          datetime(year=2009, month=5, day=2)))
        self.assertNotEqual(self.A, statuses('A',
                          datetime(year=2008, month=7, day=15),
                          datetime(year=2010, month=5, day=2)))
```

The `test_equality` test checks that a status compares equal to itself, and that differences in name, start time or end time cause statuses to compare as unequal.

```python
def test_overlap_begin(self):
    status = statuses('status name',
                      datetime(year=2007, month=8, day=11),
                      datetime(year=2008, month=11, day=27))
    self.assertTrue(status.overlaps(self.A))
def test_overlap_end(self):
    status = statuses('status name',
                      datetime(year=2008, month=1, day=11),
                      datetime(year=2010, month=4, day=16))
    self.assertTrue(status.overlaps(self.A))
def test_overlap_inner(self):
    status = statuses('status name',
                      datetime(year=2007, month=10, day=11),
                      datetime(year=2010, month=1, day=27))
    self.assertTrue(status.overlaps(self.A))
def test_overlap_outer(self):
    status = statuses('status name',
                      datetime(year=2008, month=8, day=12),
                      datetime(year=2008, month=9, day=15))
    self.assertTrue(status.overlaps(self.A))
def test_overlap_after(self):
    status = statuses('status name',
                      datetime(year=2011, month=2, day=6),
                      datetime(year=2015, month=4, day=27))
    self.assertFalse(status.overlaps(self.A))
```

This series of tests checks that statuses correctly recognize when they overlap, whether that overlap happens at the beginning, at the end, or because one status is within the other.

```python
class activities_integration_tests(TestCase):
    def setUp(self):
        self.A = activities('A',
                            datetime(year=2008, month=7, day=15),
                            datetime(year=2009, month=5, day=2))
    def test_repr(self):
        self.assertEqual(repr(self.A), '<A 2008-07-15T00:00:00
2009-05-02T00:00:00>')
    def test_equality(self):
        self.assertEqual(self.A, self.A)
        self.assertNotEqual(self.A, activities('B',
                            datetime(year=2008, month=7, day=15),
```

```
                                datetime(year=2009, month=5, day=2)))
            self.assertNotEqual(self.A, activities('A',
                                datetime(year=2007, month=7, day=15),
                                datetime(year=2009, month=5, day=2)))
            self.assertNotEqual(self.A, activities('A',
                                datetime(year=2008, month=7, day=15),
                                datetime(year=2010, month=5, day=2)))
```

As with statuses, activities are tested by creating a sample object in the `setUp` method, and performing operations on it in the tests. Equality checking is the same as in statuses; we want to make sure that a different name, begin time, or end time means that the two activities are not equal.

```
    def test_overlap_begin(self):
        activity = activities('activity name',
                                datetime(year=2007, month=8, day=11),
                                datetime(year=2008, month=11, day=27))

        self.assertTrue(activity.overlaps(self.A))
        self.assertTrue(activity.excludes(self.A))
    def test_overlap_end(self):
        activity = activities('activity name',
                                datetime(year=2008, month=1, day=11),
                                datetime(year=2010, month=4, day=16))

        self.assertTrue(activity.overlaps(self.A))
        self.assertTrue(activity.excludes(self.A))
    def test_overlap_inner(self):
        activity = activities('activity name',
                                datetime(year=2007, month=10, day=11),
                                datetime(year=2010, month=1, day=27))

        self.assertTrue(activity.overlaps(self.A))
        self.assertTrue(activity.excludes(self.A))
    def test_overlap_outer(self):
        activity = activities('activity name',
                                datetime(year=2008, month=8, day=12),
                                datetime(year=2008, month=9, day=15))

        self.assertTrue(activity.overlaps(self.A))
        self.assertTrue(activity.excludes(self.A))
    def test_overlap_after(self):
        activity = activities('activity name',
                                datetime(year=2011, month=2, day=6),
                                datetime(year=2015, month=4, day=27))

        self.assertFalse(activity.overlaps(self.A))
```

This series of tests makes sure that activities correctly recognize when they overlap with each other, whether that overlapping happens at the beginning, the end, or in the middle.

```
class schedules_tests(MockerTestCase):
    def setUp(self):
        mocker = self.mocker
        A = mocker.mock()
        A.__eq__(MATCH(lambda x: x is A))
        mocker.result(True)
        mocker.count(0, None)
        A.__eq__(MATCH(lambda x: x is not A))
        mocker.result(False)
        mocker.count(0, None)
        A.overlaps(ANY)
        mocker.result(False)
        mocker.count(0, None)
        A.begins
        mocker.result(5)
        mocker.count(0, None)
        B = mocker.mock()
        A.__eq__(MATCH(lambda x: x is B))
        mocker.result(True)
        mocker.count(0, None)
        B.__eq__(MATCH(lambda x: x is not B))
        mocker.result(False)
        mocker.count(0, None)
        B.overlaps(ANY)
        mocker.result(False)
        mocker.count(0, None)
        B.begins
        mocker.result(3)
        mocker.count(0, None)
        C = mocker.mock()
        C.__eq__(MATCH(lambda x: x is C))
        mocker.result(True)
        mocker.count(0, None)
        C.__eq__(MATCH(lambda x: x is not C))
        mocker.result(False)
        mocker.count(0, None)
        C.overlaps(ANY)
        mocker.result(False)
        mocker.count(0, None)
        C.begins
        mocker.result(7)
        mocker.count(0, None)
        self.A = A
        self.B = B
        self.C = C
        mocker.replay()
```

We'll test how `schedules` interacts with itself, but not yet how it interacts with `activities` and `statuses`. As such, we need some mock objects to represent those things. Here in the test fixture, we create three mock objects for just that purpose.

```python
def test_equality(self):
    sched1 = schedules()
    sched2 = schedules()
    self.assertEqual(sched1, sched2)
    sched1.add(self.A)
    sched1.add(self.B)

    sched2.add(self.A)
    sched2.add(self.B)
    sched2.add(self.C)
    self.assertNotEqual(sched1, sched2)
    sched1.add(self.C)
    self.assertEqual(sched1, sched2)
```

The only interaction that `schedules` has with itself is equality comparison, so here we've tested that the comparison between two real schedules works the way it's supposed to.

```python
class test_schedules_and_statuses(TestCase):
    def setUp(self):
        self.A = statuses('A',
                          datetime.now(),
                          datetime.now() + timedelta(minutes = 7))
        self.B = statuses('B',
                          datetime.now() - timedelta(hours = 1),
                          datetime.now() + timedelta(hours = 1))
        self.C = statuses('C',
                          datetime.now() + timedelta(minutes = 10),
                          datetime.now() + timedelta(hours = 1))
```

Where before we used mock objects to represent the statuses, now we can use the real thing. Since we're testing the interaction between `schedules` and `statuses`, we *need* to use the real thing.

```python
def test_usage_pattern(self):
    sched = schedules()
    sched.add(self.A)
    sched.add(self.C)
    self.assertTrue(self.A in sched)
    self.assertTrue(self.C in sched)
    self.assertFalse(self.B in sched)
    sched.add(self.B)
    self.assertTrue(self.B in sched)
    self.assertEqual(sched, sched)
```

```
        sched.remove(self.A)
        self.assertFalse(self.A in sched)
        self.assertTrue(self.B in sched)
        self.assertTrue(self.C in sched)
        sched.remove(self.B)
        sched.remove(self.C)
        self.assertFalse(self.B in sched)
        self.assertFalse(self.C in sched)
```

This test runs through the whole expected usage pattern between `schedules` and `statuses`, all in one test. This sort of thing isn't a good idea when we perform unit testing, because it naturally involves more than one unit. We're doing integration testing now, though, and all of the involved units have already been tested in isolation. We actually want to have them interact with each other to make sure it works, and this is a good way to achieve that.

```
    class test_schedules_and_activities(TestCase):
        def setUp(self):
            self.A = activities('A',
                                datetime.now(),
                                datetime.now() + timedelta(minutes = 7))
            self.B = activities('B',
                                datetime.now() - timedelta(hours = 1),
                                datetime.now() + timedelta(hours = 1))
            self.C = activities('C',
                                datetime.now() + timedelta(minutes = 10),
                                datetime.now() + timedelta(hours = 1))
        def test_usage_pattern(self):
            sched = schedules()
            sched.add(self.A)
            sched.add(self.C)
            self.assertTrue(self.A in sched)
            self.assertTrue(self.C in sched)
            self.assertFalse(self.B in sched)
            self.assertRaises(schedule_error, sched.add, self.B)
            self.assertFalse(self.B in sched)
            self.assertEqual(sched, sched)
            sched.remove(self.A)
            self.assertFalse(self.A in sched)
            self.assertFalse(self.B in sched)
            self.assertTrue(self.C in sched)
            sched.remove(self.C)
            self.assertFalse(self.B in sched)
            self.assertFalse(self.C in sched)
```

These tests are a lot like the tests for `schedules` and `statuses` together. The differences are due to the fact that activities can exclude each other from participating in a schedule, so when we try to add an overlapping activity to the schedule, it should raise an exception, and then should not be added to the schedule.

```python
class test_schedules_activities_and_statuses(TestCase):
    def setUp(self):
        self.A = statuses('A',
                          datetime.now(),
                          datetime.now() + timedelta(minutes = 7))
        self.B = statuses('B',
                          datetime.now() - timedelta(hours = 1),
                          datetime.now() + timedelta(hours = 1))
        self.C = statuses('C',
                          datetime.now() + timedelta(minutes = 10),
                          datetime.now() + timedelta(hours = 1))
        self.D = activities('D',
                            datetime.now(),
                            datetime.now() + timedelta(minutes = 7))
        self.E = activities('E',
                            datetime.now() + timedelta(minutes=30),
                            datetime.now() + timedelta(hours=1))
        self.F = activities('F',
                            datetime.now() - timedelta(minutes=20),
                            datetime.now() + timedelta(minutes=40))
```

We're not using any mocks at all here. These tests use `schedules`, `activities`, and `statuses` without any limits on their interactions. Our test fixture just creates a bunch of them, so we don't have to duplicate that code in each of the tests.

```python
    def test_usage_pattern(self):
        sched = schedules()
        sched.add(self.A)
        sched.add(self.B)
        sched.add(self.C)
        sched.add(self.D)
        self.assertTrue(self.A in sched)
        self.assertTrue(self.B in sched)
        self.assertTrue(self.C in sched)
        self.assertTrue(self.D in sched)
        self.assertRaises(schedule_error, sched.add, self.F)
        self.assertFalse(self.F in sched)
        sched.add(self.E)
        sched.remove(self.D)
        self.assertTrue(self.E in sched)
        self.assertFalse(self.D in sched)
        self.assertRaises(schedule_error, sched.add, self.F)
```

```
        self.assertFalse(self.F in sched)
        sched.remove(self.E)
        self.assertFalse(self.E in sched)
        sched.add(self.F)
        self.assertTrue(self.F in sched)
```

Here again, we have a single test for a complete usage pattern. We're intentionally not limiting the interactions between the tested components; instead we're putting them together and making sure that they work.

```
class test_file(TestCase):
    def setUp(self):
        storage = file('file_test.sqlite')
        storage.store_object('tag1', 'A')
        storage.store_object('tag2', 'B')
        storage.store_object('tag1', 'C')
        storage.store_object('tag1', 'D')
        storage.store_object('tag3', 'E')
        storage.store_object('tag3', 'F')
    def tearDown(self):
        unlink('file_test.sqlite')
```

Our test fixture creates a persistence database, containing several objects before each test runs, and deletes that database after each test. As usual, that means we know what the environment looks like for each test, and they don't interact with each other.

```
    def test_other_instance(self):
        storage = file('file_test.sqlite')
        self.assertEqual(set(storage.load_objects('tag1')),
                         set(['A', 'C', 'D']))
        self.assertEqual(set(storage.load_objects('tag2')),
                         set(['B']))
        self.assertEqual(set(storage.load_objects('tag3')),
                         set(['E', 'F']))
```

In this test, we create a new persistence file object, and tell it to load data from the database created in the setUp method. Then we make sure that the loaded data match our expectations.

When we run this test, it turns up an error which was not previously visible. The changes to the database aren't being committed to the file, and so they aren't visible outside of the transaction where they were stored. Not testing the persistence code in separate transactions was an oversight, but that's exactly the sort of mistake that we perform integration testing to catch.

We can fix the problem by altering the `store_object` method of the `file` class in `persistence.py` as follows:

```python
    def store_object(self, tag, object):
        self.connection.execute('insert into objects values (?, ?)',
                                (tag, sqlite3.Binary(dumps(object))))
        self.connection.commit()
def unpickle_mocked_task(begins):
    mocker = Mocker()
    ret = mocker.mock()
    ret.overlaps(ANY)
    mocker.result(False)
    mocker.count(0, None)
    ret.begins
    mocker.result(begins)
    mocker.count(0, None)
    mocker.replay()
    return ret
unpickle_mocked_task.__safe_for_unpickling__ = True
```

The `unpickle_mocked_task` function is necessary because one thing that mocks doesn't handle very well is being 'pickled' and 'unpickled'. We used tuples in the tests for `file` because of that, but we need mocks for this test, so we have to go to the extra trouble of telling Pickle how to handle them.

```python
class test_schedules_and_file(MockerTestCase):
    def setUp(self):
        mocker = self.mocker

        A = mocker.mock()
        A.overlaps(ANY)
        mocker.result(False)
        mocker.count(0, None)
        A.begins
        mocker.result(5)
        mocker.count(0, None)
        A.__reduce_ex__(ANY)
        mocker.result((unpickle_mocked_task, (5,)))
        mocker.count(0, None)

        B = mocker.mock()
        B.overlaps(ANY)
        mocker.result(False)
        mocker.count(0, None)
        B.begins
        mocker.result(3)
        mocker.count(0, None)
        B.__reduce_ex__(ANY)
        mocker.result((unpickle_mocked_task, (3,)))
        mocker.count(0, None)

        C = mocker.mock()
```

```
            C.overlaps(ANY)
            mocker.result(False)
            mocker.count(0, None)
            C.begins
            mocker.result(7)
            mocker.count(0, None)
            C.__reduce_ex__(ANY)
            mocker.result((unpickle_mocked_task, (7,)))
            mocker.count(0, None)
            self.A = A
            self.B = B
            self.C = C
            mocker.replay()
        def tearDown(self):
            try:
                unlink('test_schedules_and_file.sqlite')
            except OSError:
                pass
```

This should be a fairly familiar sort of test fixture, by now. The new thing is that the tearDown method will delete a database file, (if it exists) but won't complain if it doesn't. The database is expected to be created within the test itself, and we don't want to leave it lying around, but if it's not there, it's not a test fixture error.

```
        def test_save_and_restore(self):
            sched1 = schedules()
            sched1.add(self.A)
            sched1.add(self.B)
            sched1.add(self.C)
            store1 = file('test_schedules_and_file.sqlite')
            sched1.store(store1)
            del sched1
            del store1
            store2 = file('test_schedules_and_file.sqlite')
            sched2 = schedules.load(store2)
            self.assertEqual(set([x.begins for x in sched2.tasks]),
                             set([3, 5, 7]))
```

We're testing the interaction between schedules and persistence files, which means we've created and populated a schedule, created a persistence file, stored the schedule, and then created a new persistence file object using the same database file and loaded a new schedule from it. If the loaded schedule matches our expectations, all's well.

A lot of the test code in this chapter might seem redundant to you. That's because, in some sense, it is. Some things are repeatedly checked in different tests. Why bother?

The main reason for the redundancy is that each test is supposed to stand alone. We're not supposed to care what order they run in, or whether any other tests even exist. Each test is self-contained, so if it fails, we know exactly what needs to be fixed. Because each test is self-contained, some foundational things end up getting tested multiple times. In the case of this simple project, that redundancy is even more pronounced than it would normally be.

Whether it's blatant or subtle, the redundancy isn't a problem. The so-called DRY (Don't Repeat Yourself) principle doesn't particularly apply to tests. There's not much downside to having something tested multiple times. This is not to say that it's a good idea to copy and paste tests, because it's most certainly not. Don't be surprised or alarmed to see similarity between your tests, but don't use that as an excuse.

Pop quiz – writing integration tests

1. Which integration tests do you write first?
2. What happens when you have a large chunk of integrated code, but the next section you need to pull in doesn't have any integration tests at all?
3. What's the point of writing tests that check the integration of a chunk of code with itself?
4. What is a system test, and how do system tests relate to integration tests?

Have a go hero – integrating your own program

Earlier, you wrote an integration diagram for one of your own programs. It's time now to follow up on that and write integration tests for that code, guided by the diagram.

Summary

In this chapter, we learned about the process of building up from a foundation of unit tests, into a set of tests that cover the whole system.

Specifically, we covered:

- How to draw an integration diagram
- How to interpret an integration diagram to decide in what order to build the tests
- How to write integration tests

Now that we've learned about integration testing, we're ready to introduce a number of other useful testing tools and strategies—which is the topic of the next chapter.

10
Other Testing Tools and Techniques

We've covered the core elements of testing in Python, but there are a number of peripheral methods and tools that will make your life easier. In this chapter, we'll go over several of them in brief.

In this chapter, we shall:

- ◆ Discuss code coverage, and learn about `coverage.py`
- ◆ Discuss continuous integration, and learn about buildbot
- ◆ Learn how to integrate automated testing into popular version control systems

So let's get on with it!

Code coverage

Tests tell you when the code you're testing doesn't work the way you thought it would, but they don't tell you a thing about the code that you're *not* testing. They don't even tell you that the code you're not testing isn't being tested.

Code coverage is a technique, which can be used to address that shortcoming. A code coverage tool watches while your tests are running, and keeps track of which lines of code are (and aren't) executed. After the tests have run, the tool will give you a report describing how well your tests cover the whole body of code.

It's desirable to have the coverage approach 100%, as you probably figured out already. Be careful not to focus on the coverage number too intensely though, it can be a bit misleading. Even if your tests execute every line of code in the program, they can easily not test everything that needs to be tested. That means you can't take 100% coverage as certain proof that your tests are complete. On the other hand, there are times when some code really, truly doesn't need to be covered by the tests—some debugging support code, for example—and so less than 100% coverage can be completely acceptable.

Code coverage is a tool to give you insight into what your tests are doing, and what they may be overlooking. It's not the definition of a good test suite.

coverage.py

We're going to be working with a module called `coverage.py`, which is—unsurprisingly—a code coverage tool for Python.

Since `coverage.py` isn't built in to Python, we'll need to download and install it. You can download the latest version from the Python Package Index at `http://pypi.python.org/pypi/coverage`. As before, users of Python 2.6 or later can install the package by unpacking the archive, changing to the directory, and typing:

```
$ python setup.py install --user
```

> Users of older versions of Python need write permission to the system-wide `site-packages` directory, which is part of the Python installation. Anybody who has such permission can install coverage by typing:
>
> `$ python setup.py install`
>
> At the time of this writing, Windows users also had the option of downloading a Windows installer file from the Python Package Index and running it to install `coverage.py`.

We'll walk through the steps of using `coverage.py` here, but if you want more information you can find it on the `coverage.py` home page at `http://nedbatchelder.com/code/coverage/`.

Time for action – using coverage.py

We'll create a little `toy` code module with tests, and then apply `coverage.py` to find out how much of the code the tests actually use.

1. Place the following test code into `test_toy.py`. There are several problems with these tests, which we'll discuss later, but they ought to run.

```
from unittest import TestCase
import toy

class test_global_function(TestCase):
    def test_positive(self):
        self.assertEqual(toy.global_function(3), 4)

    def test_negative(self):
        self.assertEqual(toy.global_function(-3), -2)

    def test_large(self):
        self.assertEqual(toy.global_function(2**13), 2**13 + 1)

class test_example_class(TestCase):
    def test_timestwo(self):
        example = toy.example_class(5)
        self.assertEqual(example.timestwo(), 10)

    def test_repr(self):
        example = toy.example_class(7)
        self.assertEqual(repr(example), '<example param="7">')
```

2. Put the following code into `toy.py`. Notice the `if __name__ == '__main__'` clause at the bottom. We haven't dealt with one of those in a while, so I'll remind you that the code inside that block runs doctest if we were to run the module with `python toy.py`.

```
def global_function(x):
    r"""
    >>> global_function(5)
    6
    """
    return x + 1

class example_class:
    def __init__(self, param):
        self.param = param

    def timestwo(self):
        return self.param * 2

    def __repr__(self):
        return '<example param="%s">' % self.param
```

```
if __name__ == '__main__':
    import doctest
    doctest.testmod()
```

3. Go ahead and run Nose. It should find them, run them, and report that all is well. The problem is, some of the code isn't ever tested.

4. Let's run it again, only this time we'll tell Nose to use `coverage.py` to measure coverage while it's running the tests.

```
$ nosetests --with-coverage --cover-erase
```

```
Name    Stmts    Exec   Cover   Missing
-----------------------------------------
toy        12       9    75%    16, 19-20
-----------------------------------------
Ran 5 tests in 0.037s

OK
```

What just happened?

In step 1, we have a couple of `TestCase` classes with some very basic tests in them. These tests wouldn't be much use in a real world situation, but all we need them for is to illustrate how the code coverage tool works.

In step 2, we have the code that satisfies the tests from step 1. Like the tests themselves, this code wouldn't be much use, but it serves as an illustration.

In step 4, we passed `--with-coverage` and `--cover-erase` as command line parameters when we ran Nose. What did they do? Well, `--with-coverage` is pretty straightforward: it told Nose to look for `coverage.py` and to use it while the tests execute. That's just what we wanted. The second parameter, `--cover-erase`, tells Nose to forget about any coverage information that was acquired during previous runs. By default, coverage information is aggregated across all of the uses of `coverage.py`. This allows you to run a set of tests using different testing frameworks or mechanisms, and then check the cumulative coverage. You still want to erase the data from previous test runs at the beginning of that process, though, and the `--cover-erase` command line is how you tell Nose to tell `coverage.py` that you're starting anew.

What the coverage report tells us is that 9/12 (in other words, 75%) of the executable statements in the toy module were executed during our tests, and that the missing lines were line 16 and a lines 19 through 20. Looking back at our code, we see that line 16 is the `__repr__` method. We really should have tested that, so the coverage check has revealed a hole in our tests that we should fix. Lines 19 and 20 are just code to run doctest, though. They're not something that we ought to be using under normal circumstances, so we can just ignore that coverage hole.

Code coverage can't detect problems with the tests themselves, in most cases. In the above test code, the test for the `timestwo` method violates the isolation of units and invokes two different methods of `example_class`. Since one of the methods is the constructor, this may be acceptable, but the coverage checker isn't in a position to even see that there might be a problem. All it saw was more lines of code being covered. That's not a problem— it's how a coverage checker ought to work— but it's something to keep in mind. Coverage is useful, but high coverage doesn't equal good tests.

Pop quiz – code coverage

1. What does a high coverage percentage mean?
2. If your boss asks you for a quantifiable measure of test quality, will you use the coverage percentage?
3. What is the most useful information on the coverage report?

Have a go hero – checking coverage in earlier chapters

Go back through the code from earlier chapters and use code coverage to check for things that should have been tested, but weren't. Try it on some of your own tested code too.

Version control hooks

Most version control systems have the ability to run a program that you've written in response to various events, as a way of customizing the version control system's behavior. These programs are commonly called hooks.

Version control systems are programs for keeping track of changes to a source code tree, even when those changes are made by different people. In a sense, they provide an universal undo history and change log for the whole project, going all the way back to the moment you started using the version control system. They also make it much easier to combine work done by different people into a single, unified entity, and to keep track of different editions of the same project.

You can do all kinds of things by installing the right hook programs, but we'll only focus on one use. We can make the version control program automatically run our tests, when we commit a new version of the code to the version control repository.

This is a fairly nifty trick, because it makes it difficult for test-breaking bugs to get into the repository unnoticed. Somewhat like code coverage, though there's potential for trouble if it becomes a matter of policy rather than simply being a tool to make your life easier.

In most systems, you can write the hooks such that it's impossible to commit code that breaks tests. That may sound like a good idea at first, but it's really not. One reason for this is that one of the major purposes of a version control system is communication between developers, and interfering with that tends to be unproductive in the long run. Another reason is that it prevents anybody from committing partial solutions to problems, which means that things tend to get dumped into the repository in big chunks. Big commits are a problem because they make it hard to keep track of what changed, which adds to the confusion. There are better ways to make sure you always have a working codebase socked away somewhere, such as version control branches.

Bazaar

Bazaar is a distributed version control system, which means that it is capable of operating without a central server or master copy of the source code. One consequence of the distributed nature of Bazaar is that each user has their own set of hooks, which can be added, modified, or removed without involving anyone else. Bazaar is available on the Internet at http://bazaar-vcs.org/.

If you don't have Bazaar already installed, and don't plan on using it, you can skip this section.

Time for action – installing Nose as a Bazaar post-commit hook

1. Bazaar hooks go in your `plugins` directory. On Unix-like systems, that's `~/.bazaar/plugins/`, while on Windows it's `C:\Documents and Settings\ <username>\Application Data\Bazaar\<version>\plugins\`. In either case, you may have to create the `plugins` subdirectory, if it doesn't already exist.

2. Place the following code into a file called `run_nose.py` in the `plugins` directory. Bazaar hooks are written in Python:

```python
from bzrlib import branch
from os.path import join, sep
from os import chdir
from subprocess import call

def run_nose(local, master, old_num, old_id, new_num, new_id):
    try:
        base = local.base
    except AttributeError:
        base = master.base

    if not base.startswith('file://'):
        return
```

```
try:
    chdir(join(sep, *base[7:].split('/')))
except OSError:
    return

call(['nosetests'])
branch.Branch.hooks.install_named_hook('post_commit',
                                        run_nose,
                                        'Runs Nose after each
                                         commit')
```

3. Make a new directory in your working files, and put the following code into it in a file called `test_simple.py`. These simple (and silly) tests are just to give Nose something to do, so that we can see that the hook is working.

```python
from unittest import TestCase

class test_simple(TestCase):
    def test_one(self):
        self.assertNotEqual("Testing", "Hooks")

    def test_two(self):
        self.assertEqual("Same", "Same")
```

4. Still in the same directory as `test_simple.py`, run the following commands to create a new repository and commit the tests to it. The output you see might differ in details, but it should be quite similar overall.

```
$ bzr init
$ bzr add
$ bzr commit
```

```
$ bzr init
Created a standalone tree (format: pack-0.92)
$ bzr add
adding test_simple.py
ignored 1 file(s).
If you wish to add some of these files, please add them by name.
$ bzr commit
Committing to: /home/djarb/tmp/bzr/
added test_simple.py
Committed revision 1.
..
-----------------------------------------------------------
Ran 2 tests in 0.012s

OK
```

5. Notice that there's a Nose test report after the commit notification. From now on, any time you commit to a Bazaar repository, Nose will search for and run whatever tests it can find within that repository.

What just happened?

Bazaar hooks are written in Python, so we've written our hook as a function called `run_nose`. Our `run_nose` function checks to make sure that the repository which we're working on is local, and then it changes directories into the repository and runs nose. We registered `run_nose` as a hook by calling `branch.Branch.hooks.install_named_hook`.

Mercurial

Like Bazaar, Mercurial is a distributed version control system, with hooks that are managed by each user individually. Mercurial's hooks themselves, though, take a rather different form. You can find Mercurial on the web at `http://www.selenic.com/mercurial/`.

If you don't have Mercurial installed and don't plan to use it, you can skip this section.

Mercurial hooks can go in several different places. The two most useful are in your personal configuration file and in your repository configuration file.

Your personal configuration file is `~/.hgrc` on Unix-like systems, and `%USERPROFILE%\Mercurial.ini` (which usually means `c:\Documents and Settings\<username>\Mercurial.ini`) on Windows-based systems.

Your repository configuration file is stored in a subdirectory of the repository, specifically `.hg/hgrc`, on all systems.

Time for action – installing Nose as a Mercurial post-commit hook

1. We'll use the repository configuration file to store the hook, which means that the first thing we have to do is have a repository to work with. Make a new directory at a convenient place and execute the following command in it:

   ```
   $ hg init
   ```

2. One side-effect of that command is that a `.hg` subdirectory got created. Change to that directory, and then create a text file called `hgrc` containing the following text:

   ```
   [hooks]
   commit = nosetests
   ```

3. Back in the repository directory (i.e. the parent of the `.hg` directory), we need some tests for Nose to run. Create a file called `test_simple.py` containing the following (admittedly silly) tests:

```
from unittest import TestCase
class test_simple(TestCase):
    def test_one(self):
        self.assertNotEqual("Testing", "Hooks")
    def test_two(self):
        self.assertEqual("Same", "Same")
```

4. Run the following commands to add the test file and commit it to the repository:

```
$ hg add
```

```
$ hg commit
```

```
$ hg add
adding test_simple.py
$ hg commit
..
----------------------------------------
Ran 2 tests in 0.020s

OK
```

5. Notice that the commit triggered a run-through of the tests. Since we put the hook in the repository configuration file, it will only take effect on commits to this repository. If we'd instead put it into your personal configuration file, it would be called when you committed to *any* repository.

What just happened?

Mercurial's hooks are commands, just like you would enter into your operating systems command shell (also known as a DOS prompt on Windows). We just had to edit Mercurial's configuration file and tell it which command to run. Since we wanted it to run our Nose test suite when we commit, we set the commit hook to `nosetests`.

Git

Git is a distributed version control system. Similar to Bazaar and Mercurial, it allows every user to control their own hooks, without involving other developers or server administrators.

 Git hooks are stored in the `.git/hooks/` subdirectory of the repository, each in its own file.

If you don't have Git installed, and don't plan to use it, you can skip this section.

Time for action – installing Nose as a Git post-commit hook

1. The hooks are stored in a subdirectory of a Git repository, so the first thing that we need to do is initialize a repository. Make a new directory for the Git repository and execute the following command inside of it:

```
$ git init
```

2. Git hooks are executable programs, so they can be written in any language. To run Nose, it makes sense to use a shell script (on Unix-like systems) or batch file (on Windows) for the hook. If you're using a Unix-like system, place the following two lines into a file called post-commit in the .git/hooks/ subdirectory, and then use the `chmod +x post-commit` command to make it executable.

```
#!/bin/sh
nosetests
```

If you're using a Windows system, place the following lines inside a file called `post-commit.bat` in the .git\hooks\ subdirectory.

```
@echo off
nosetests
```

3. We need to put some test code in the repository directory (that is, the parent of the .git directory), so that Nose has something to do. Place the following (useless) code into a file called test_simple.py:

```
from unittest import TestCase

class test_simple(TestCase):
    def test_one(self):
        self.assertNotEqual("Testing", "Hooks")

    def test_two(self):
        self.assertEqual("Same", "Same")
```

4. Run the following commands to add the test file and commit it to the repository:

```
$ git add test_simple.py
$ git commit -a
```

```
$ git add test_simple.py
$ git commit -a
..
----------------------------------------------------------------
Ran 2 tests in 0.056s

OK
[master (root-commit) 8c7790d] initial
 1 files changed, 8 insertions(+), 0 deletions(-)
 create mode 100644 test_simple.py
```

5. Notice that the commit triggered an execution of Nose and printed out the test results.

Because each repository has its own hooks, only the repositories that were specifically configured to run Nose will do so.

What just happened?

Git finds its hooks by looking for programs with specific names, so we could have used any programming language to write our hook, as long as we could give the program the right name. However, all that we want is to run the `nosetests` command, so that we can use a simple shell script or batch file. All this simple program does is invoke the `nosetests` program, and then terminate.

Darcs

Darcs is a distributed version control system. Each user has control over their own set of hooks.

If you don't have Darcs installed, and you don't plan to use it, you can skip this section.

Time for action – installing Nose as a Darcs post-record hook

1. Each local repository has its own set of hooks, so the first thing we need to do is create a repository. Make a directory to work in, and execute the following command in it:

```
$ darcs initialize
```

2. We need to put some test code in the repository directory so that Nose has something to do. Place the following (useless) code into a file called `test_simple.py`.

```
from unittest import TestCase

class test_simple(TestCase):
    def test_one(self):
        self.assertNotEqual("Testing", "Hooks")

    def test_two(self):
        self.assertEqual("Same", "Same")
```

3. Run the following command to add the test file to the repository:

```
$ darcs add test_simple.py
```

4. Darcs hooks are identified using command line options. In this case, we want to run `nosetests` after we tell Darcs to record changes, so we use the following command:

```
$ darcs record --posthook=nosetests
```

```
$ darcs add test_simple.py
$ darcs record --posthook=nosetests
addfile ./test_simple.py
Shall I record this change? (1/2)  [ynWsfvpxdaqjk], or ? for help: y
hunk ./test_simple.py 1
+from unittest import TestCase
+
+class test_simple(TestCase):
+    def test_one(self):
+        self.assertNotEqual("Testing", "Hooks")
+
+    def test_two(self):
+        self.assertEqual("Same", "Same")
Shall I record this change? (2/2)  [ynWsfvpxdaqjk], or ? for help: y
What is the patch name? initial
Do you want to add a long comment? [yn]n
Finished recording patch 'initial'

The following command is set to execute.
Execute the following command now (yes or no)?
nosetests
yes
..
----------------------------------------------------------------------
Ran 2 tests in 0.013s

OK
```

5. Notice that Darcs ran our test suite once it was done recording the changes, and reported the results to us.

6. That's well and good, but Darcs doesn't remember that we want `nosetests` to be a post-record hook. As far as it's concerned, that was a one-time deal. Fortunately, we can tell it otherwise. Create a file called `defaults` in the `_darcs/prefs/` subdirectory, and place the following text into it:

```
record posthook nosetests
```

7. Now if we change the code and record again, `nosetests` should run without us specifically asking for it. Make the following change to `test_simple.py`:

```
from unittest import TestCase

class test_simple(TestCase):
    def test_one(self):
        self.assertNotEqual("Testing", "Hooks")

    def test_two(self):
        self.assertEqual("Same", "Same!")
```

8. Run the following command to record the change and run the tests:

`darcs record`

```
$ darcs record
hunk ./test_simple.py 8
-        self.assertEqual("Same", "Same")
+        self.assertEqual("Same", "Same!")
Shall I record this change? (1/1)  [ynWsfvpxdaqjk], or ? for help: y
What is the patch name? broke it
Do you want to add a long comment? [yn]n
Finished recording patch 'broke it'

The following command is set to execute.
Execute the following command now (yes or no)?
nosetests
yes
.F
=====================================================================
FAIL: test_two (test_simple.test_simple)
---------------------------------------------------------------------
Traceback (most recent call last):
  File "/home/djarb/tmp/darcs/test_simple.py", line 8, in test_two
    self.assertEqual("Same", "Same!")
AssertionError: 'Same' != 'Same!'

---------------------------------------------------------------------
Ran 2 tests in 0.013s

FAILED (failures=1)
Posthook failed!
```

9. If you want to skip the tests for a commit, you can pass the `--no-posthook` command line option when you record your changes.

What just happened?

Darcs hooks are specified as command line options, so when we issue the `record` command we need to specify a program to run as a hook. Since we don't want to do that manually every time we record changes, we make use of Darcs' ability to accept additional command line options in its configuration file. This allows us to make running `nosetests` as a hook into the default behavior.

Subversion

Unlike the other version control systems that we've discussed, Subversion is a centralized one. There is a single server tasked with keeping track of everybody's changes, which also handles running hooks. This means that there is a single set of hooks that applies to everybody, probably under control of a system administrator.

 Subversion hooks are stored in files in the `hooks/` subdirectory of the server's repository.

If you don't have Subversion and don't plan on using it, you can skip this section.

Time for action – installing Nose as a Subversion post-commit hook

Because Subversion operates on an centralized, client-server architecture, we'll need both the client and server set up for this example. They can both be on the same computer, but they'll need to be in different directories.

1. First we need a server. You can create one by making a new directory called svnrepo and executing the following command:

    ```
    $ svnadmin create svnrepo/
    ```

2. Now we need to configure the server to accept commits from us. To do this, we open up the file called conf/passwd and add the following line at the bottom:

    ```
    testuser = testpass
    ```

3. Then we need to edit conf/svnserve.conf, and change the line reading # password-db = passwd to password-db = passwd.

4. The Subversion server needs to be running, before we can interact with it. This is done by making sure that we're in the svnrepo directory and then running the following command:

    ```
    svnserve -d -r ..
    ```

5. Next we need to import some test code into the Subversion repository. Make a directory and place the following (simple and silly) code into it in a file called test_simple.py:

    ```
    from unittest import TestCase

    class test_simple(TestCase):
        def test_one(self):
            self.assertNotEqual("Testing", "Hooks")

        def test_two(self):
            self.assertEqual("Same", "Same")
    ```

    You can perform the import by executing:

    ```
    $ svn import --username=testuser --password=testpass svn://
    localhost/svnrepo/
    ```

    That command is likely to print out a gigantic, scary message about remembering passwords. In spite of the warnings, just say yes.

6. Now that we've got the code imported, we need to check out a copy of it to work on. We can do this with the following command:

```
$ svn checkout --username=testuser --password=testpass svn://
localhost/svnrepo/ svn
```

 From here on in this example, we'll assume that the Subversion server is running in a Unix-like environment (the clients might be running on Windows, we don't care). The reason for this, is that the details of the post-commit hook are significantly different on systems that don't have a Unix style shell scripting language, although the concepts remain the same.

7. The following code goes into a file called hooks/post-commit inside the subversion server's repository. (The svn update and svn checkout lines have been wrapped around to fit on the page. In actual use, this wrapping should not be present.)

```
#!/bin/sh
REPO="$1"

if /usr/bin/test -e "$REPO/working"; then
    /usr/bin/svn update --username=testuser --password=testpass
"$REPO/working/";
else
    /usr/bin/svn checkout --username=testuser --password=testpass
svn://localhost/svnrepo/ "$REPO/working/";
fi

cd "$REPO/working/"

exec /usr/bin/nosetests
```

8. Use the chmod +x post-commit command to make the hook executable.

9. Change to the svn directory created by the checkout in step 5, and edit test_simple.py to make one of the tests fail. We do this because if the tests all pass, Subversion won't show us anything to indicate that they were run at all. We only get feedback if they fail.

```
from unittest import TestCase

class test_simple(TestCase):
    def test_one(self):
        self.assertNotEqual("Testing", "Hooks")

    def test_two(self):
        self.assertEqual("Same", "Same!")
```

10. Now commit the changes using the following command:

```
$ svn commit --username=testuser --password=testpass
```

```
$ svn commit --username=testuser --password=testpass
Sending        test_simple.py
Transmitting file data .
Committed revision 8.

Warning: post-commit hook failed (exit code 1) with output:
.F
======================================================================
FAIL: test_two (test_simple.test_simple)
----------------------------------------------------------------------
Traceback (most recent call last):
  File "/home/djarb/tmp/svnrepo/working/test_simple.py", line 8, in test_two
    self.assertEqual("Same", "Same!")
AssertionError: 'Same' != 'Same!'

----------------------------------------------------------------------
Ran 2 tests in 0.014s

FAILED (failures=1)
```

11. Notice that the commit triggered the execution of Nose, and that if any of the tests fail, Subversion shows us the errors.

Because Subversion has one central set of hooks, they apply automatically to anybody who uses the repository.

What just happened?

Subversion hooks are run on the server. Subversion locates its hooks by looking for programs with specific names, so we needed to create a program called `post-commit` to be the post-commit hook. We could have used any programming language to write the hook, as long as the program had the right name, but we chose to use shell scripting language, for simplicity's sake.

Pop quiz – version control hooks

1. In what ways can hooking your automated tests into your version control system help you?

2. What are a couple of the things you could do with version control hooks, but shouldn't?

3. What is the biggest difference between hooks in distributed version control systems, and hooks in centralized version control systems?

Automated continuous integration

Automated continuous integration tools are a step beyond using a version control hook to run your tests when you commit code to the repository. Instead of running your test suite once, an automated continuous integration system compiles your code (if need be) and runs your tests many times, in many different environments.

An automated continuous integration system might, for example, run your tests under Python versions 2.4, 2.5, and 2.6 on each of Windows, Linux, and Mac OS X. This not only lets you know about errors in your code, but also about unexpected problems caused by the external environment. It's nice to know when that last patch broke the program on Windows, even though it worked like a charm on your Linux box.

Buildbot

Buildbot is a popular automated continuous integration tool. Using Buildbot, you can create a network of 'build slaves' that will check your code each time you commit to you commit it to your repository. This network can be quite large, and it can be distributed around the Internet, so Buildbot works even for projects with lots of developers spread around the world.

Buildbot's home page is at `http://buildbot.net/`. Following links from that site, you can find the manual and download the latest version of the tool. Glossing over details that we've discussed several times before, installation requires you to unpack the archive, and then run the commands `python setup.py build`, and `python setup.py install --user`.

Buildbot operates in one of two modes, termed `buildmaster` and `buildslave`. A buildmaster manages a network of buildslaves, while the buildslaves run the tests in their assorted environments.

Time for action – using Buildbot with Bazaar

1. To set up a buildmaster, create a directory for it to operate in and then run the command:

    ```
    $ buildbot create-master <directory>
    ```

    where `<directory>` is the directory you just created for buildbot to work in.

2. Similarly, to set up a buildslave, create a directory for it to operate in and then run the command:

    ```
    $ buildbot create-slave <directory> <host:port> <name> <password>
    ```

where `<directory>` is the directory you just created for the buildbot to work in, `<host:port>` are the internet host and port where the buildmaster can be found, and `<name>` and `<password>` are the login information that identifies this buildslave to the buildmaster. All of this information (except the directory) is determined by the operator of the buildmaster.

3. You should edit `<directory>/info/admin` and `<directory>/info/host` to contain the email address you want associated with this buildslave and a description of the buildslave's operating environment, respectively.

4. On both the buildmaster and the buildslave, you'll need to start up the buildbot background process. To do this, use the command:

```
$ buildbot start <directory>
```

5. Configuring a buildmaster is a significant topic in itself (and one that we' won't be addressing in detail). It's fully described in Buildbot's own documentation. We will provide a simple configuration file, though, for reference and quick setup. This particular configuration file assumes that you're using Bazaar, but it is not significantly different for other version control systems. The following goes in the master `<directory>/master.cfg` file:

```python
# -*- python -*-
# ex: set syntax=python:

c = BuildmasterConfig = {}

c['projectName'] = "<replace with project name>"
c['projectURL'] = "<replace with project url>"
c['buildbotURL'] = "http://<replace with master url>:8010/"

c['status'] = []
from buildbot.status import html
c['status'].append(html.WebStatus(http_port=8010,
                                  allowForce=True))

c['slavePortnum'] = 9989

from buildbot.buildslave import BuildSlave
c['slaves'] = [
    BuildSlave("bot1name", "bot1passwd"),
    ]

from buildbot.changes.pb import PBChangeSource
c['change_source'] = PBChangeSource()

from buildbot.scheduler import Scheduler
c['schedulers'] = []
c['schedulers'].append(Scheduler(name="all", branch=None,
                                 treeStableTimer=2 * 60,
                                 builderNames=["buildbot-full"]))
```

```
from buildbot.process import factory
from buildbot.steps.source import Bzr
from buildbot.steps.shell import Test
f1 = factory.BuildFactory()
f1.addStep(Bzr(repourl="<replace with repository url>"))
f1.addStep(Test(command = 'nosetests'))

b1 = {'name': "buildbot-full",
      'slavename': "bot1name",
      'builddir': "full",
      'factory': f1,
      }
c['builders'] = [b1]
```

6. To make effective use of that Buildbot config, you also need to install a version control hook that notifies Buildbot of changes. Generically, this can be done by calling the `buildbot sendchange` command from the hook, but there's a nicer way to tie in with Bazaar: copy the `contrib/bzr_buildbot.py` file from the buildbot distribution archive into your Bazaar plugins directory, and then edit the `locations.conf` file, which you should find right next to the `plugins` directory. Add the following entry to `locations.conf`:

```
[<your repository path>]
buildbot_on = change
buildbot_server = <internet address of your buildmaster>
buildbot_port = 9989
```

You'll need to add similar entries for each repository that you want to be connected to buildbot.

7. Once you have the buildmaster and buildslaves configured, and have hooked buildbot into your version control system, and have started the buildmaster and buildslaves, you're in business.

What just happened?

We just set up Buildbot to run our tests, whenever it notices that our source code has been unchanged for two hours.

We told it to run the tests by adding a build step that runs nosetests:

```
f1.addStep(Test(command = 'nosetests'))
```

We told it to wait for the source code to be unchanged for two hours by adding a build scheduler:

```
c['schedulers'].append(Scheduler(name="all", branch=None,
                                 treeStableTimer=2 * 60,
                                 builderNames=["buildbot-full"]))
```

You'll be able to see a report of the Buildbot status in your web browser, by navigating to the `buildbotURL` that you configured in the `master.cfg` file. One of the most useful reports is the so-called 'waterfall' view. If the most recent commit passes the tests, you should see something similar to this:

time (PDT)	changes	Test
		build successful
		idle
		buildbot-full
		test stdio
		update stdio
14:25:33		Build 1

On the other hand, when the commit fails to pass the tests, you'll see something more like this:

time (PDT)	changes	Test
		failed test
		idle
		buildbot-full
		test failed stdio
		update stdio
14:21:32		Build 0

Either way, you'll also see a history of earlier versions, and whether or not they passed the tests, as well as who made the changes, when, and what the output of the test command looked like.

Pop quiz – Buildbot

1. What kind of projects benefit most from Buildbot and other such tools?
2. When is it better to use Buildbot, as opposed to just running Nose from a version control hook?
3. When is it worse?
4. Aside from running tests, what sort of tasks would Buildbot be useful for?

Have a go hero

This is an open-ended assignment: take what you've learned and put it to use. Try a small project first (but make it test-driven), with tests integrated into your version control system. Once you have an implementation, use code coverage to help you have a comprehensive test suite. If it makes sense for your project, use Buildbot.

Summary

We learned a lot in this chapter about code coverage and plugging our tests into the other automation systems that we use while writing software.

Specifically, we covered:

◆ What code coverage is, and what it can tell us about our tests
◆ How to run Nose automatically when our version control software detects changes in the source code
◆ How to set up the Buildbot automated continuous integration system

Now that we've learned about code coverage, version control hooks, and automated continuous integration, you're ready to tackle more or less anything. Congratulations!

Answers to Pop Quizes

Chapter 2

Pop quiz – doctest syntax

1. Test expression always start with >>>.

2. Continuation on lines always start with ...

3. The expected output begins immediately after the expression, and continues until the next blank line.

4. By using the normalize whitespace directive.

5. doctest ignores everything between the `Traceback (most recent last call)`.

6. All of the later code within the same text file can see the variable.

7. We care because tests are supposed to be isolated from each other, and if two tests use the same variable, they can influence each others' results.

8. We can represent that section with an ellipsis(`...`) in the expected output.

Chapter 3

Pop quiz – understanding units

1. 3 units exist: `__init__`, `method1` and `method2`.

2. Both `method1` and `method2` assume the correct operation of `__init__`, and additionally `method2` assumes the correct operation of `method1`.

3. Tests for `method2` would need to use a fake `method1`.

Pop quiz – unit testing during design

1. The tests we're building now are the foundation of the whole development process. The choices we make here affect everything that comes after; it's important to do it right.

2. If the people who write the specification aren't the same people who are writing the code, then it's important for the coders to start involving themselves as soon as possible, to keep the whole process within the bounds of what can usefully be done. If the specifiers are the coders, then the question is academic.

3. The big advantage is that the tests allow the code's interfaces to be test-driven, before the effort gets put into actually implementing them. The primary disadvantage is that the tests can lock in a design which might have benefitted from further evolution.

Pop quiz – unit testing

1. The test should be written before the code that will be tested, based on the expectations for that code.

2. True.

3. Tests should be run as often as possible. It is very useful to run the tests regularly while coding, as well as just before storing the code into a version control system.

4. You will spend most of you time using the output of the tests as a tool to guide you in finding and fixing errors in the code.

Chapter 4

Pop quiz – Mocker usage

1. `IN`.

2. Pass `None` as the upper bound.

3. It checks that the mocked objects were actually used in the way that we described.

Chapter 5

Pop quiz – basic unittest knowledge

1. ```
   class test_exceptions(TestCase):
       def test_ValueError(self):
           self.assertRaises(ValueError, int, '123')
   ```

2. Use the `assertAlmostEqual` method.

3. You would use `assertTrue` if none of the more specialized assertions suited your needs. You would use `fail` if you needed to express the conditions for test failure, so complex that they don't fit comfortably into a single Boolean expression.

Pop quiz – text fixtures

1. To provide each test with an identical, isolated environment.

2. Add `setUp` and/or `tearDown` methods to a `TestCase` subclass.

3. A test fixture can consist of either or both methods, so the answer is yes.

Chapter 6

Pop quiz – testing with Nose

1. put `processes=4` in your Nose configuration file.

2. add `--include="specs"` to the Nose command line.

3. `unit_tests`, `TestFiles`, and `test_files` will be recognized.

Chapter 7

Pop quiz – test-driven development

1. Because the testable specification didn't follow unit testing discipline, it didn't satisfy my need for unit tests. I had to write additional tests to fill that need. It's fine to do that, as long as I don't skimp on the real unit tests.

2. In no way. It's actually desirable to run your tests as often as possible.
   ```

3. You've lost the opportunity to give your code's planned interface a test drive before you set it in stone. You've lost the opportunity to write down your expectations without having them contaminated by the actual behavior of your first implementation. You've lost the opportunity to have the computer tell you what needs to be done to create a working implementation.

Chapter 8

Pop quiz – the Twill language

1. Whatever form was last touched by the `formvalue` command is submitted.

2. The `notfind` command.

3. Twill will report that the entire script failed, and not execute any of the later commands.

Pop quiz – browser methods

1. The value you pass as a parameter is matched against the form's name, number, and ID.

2. The `clicked` method moves the simulated input focus to a new control on the web page.

3. The `code` command checks the response code and raises an exception if it doesn't match an expected value. The `get_code` method simply returns the response code.

Chapter 9

Pop quiz – diagramming integration

1. Those units wouldn't exist within the same class if they weren't related to each other. By grouping them into their classes visually, we can take advantage of that relationship to make our diagrams more easily.

2. Usually, it saves us trouble later on. Things that are related to each other at one level are often part of the same thing at a higher level.

3. In testing, as in chemistry, it's important to change only one thing at a time. If we pull together more than two things in a single step, we've changed more than one thing, and so we can lose track of where any problems we find came from.

Pop quiz – writing integration tests

1. The ones in the smallest circles, especially if they don't have any lines pointing from themselves to other circles.

2. Start from the smallest circles involving that code, and build up step by step until you're ready to integrate it with your earlier code.

3. When we were doing unit testing, even other instances of the same class were mocked; we were concerned that *this code* did what it was supposed to, without involving anything else. Now that we're doing integration testing, we need to test that instances of the same class interact correctly with each other, or with themselves when they're allowed to retain state from one operation to the next. The two kinds of tests cover different things, so it makes sense that we would need both.

4. A system test is the final stage of integration testing. It's a test that involves the whole code base.

Chapter 10

Pop quiz – code coverage

1. It means that most of the code base was executed while running the tests.

2. That would be a bad idea, because coverage doesn't tell you anything about the quality of your tests. It's for helping you find things that need to be tested, not for telling you whether your tests are any good.

3. The most useful information that the coverage report provides is the list of lines that weren't executed, because that's what allows you to know what new tests you might want to add.

Pop quiz – version control hooks

1. It can ensure that your tests are executed frequently, and can make you immediately aware when you're checking in broken code.

2. Don't make it impossible to check in broken code. Don't make version control hooks a matter of company policy.

3. In a centralized version control system, the hooks are usually under the control of a system administrator, and executed on a server. In a distributed version control system, the hooks are usually under the control of the user, and executed on the user's computer.

Index

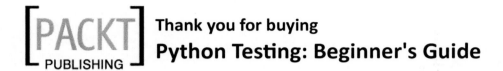

Thank you for buying
Python Testing: Beginner's Guide

Packt Open Source Project Royalties

When we sell a book written on an Open Source project, we pay a royalty directly to that project. Therefore by purchasing Python Testing: Beginner's Guide, Packt will have given some of the money received to the Python project.

In the long term, we see ourselves and you—customers and readers of our books—as part of the Open Source ecosystem, providing sustainable revenue for the projects we publish on. Our aim at Packt is to establish publishing royalties as an essential part of the service and support a business model that sustains Open Source.

If you're working with an Open Source project that you would like us to publish on, and subsequently pay royalties to, please get in touch with us.

Writing for Packt

We welcome all inquiries from people who are interested in authoring. Book proposals should be sent to author@packtpub.com. If your book idea is still at an early stage and you would like to discuss it first before writing a formal book proposal, contact us; one of our commissioning editors will get in touch with you.

We're not just looking for published authors; if you have strong technical skills but no writing experience, our experienced editors can help you develop a writing career, or simply get some additional reward for your expertise.

About Packt Publishing

Packt, pronounced 'packed', published its first book "Mastering phpMyAdmin for Effective MySQL Management" in April 2004 and subsequently continued to specialize in publishing highly focused books on specific technologies and solutions.

Our books and publications share the experiences of your fellow IT professionals in adapting and customizing today's systems, applications, and frameworks. Our solution-based books give you the knowledge and power to customize the software and technologies you're using to get the job done. Packt books are more specific and less general than the IT books you have seen in the past. Our unique business model allows us to bring you more focused information, giving you more of what you need to know, and less of what you don't.

Packt is a modern, yet unique publishing company, which focuses on producing quality, cutting-edge books for communities of developers, administrators, and newbies alike. For more information, please visit our website: www.PacktPub.com.

Expert Python Programming

ISBN: 978-1-847194-94-7   Paperback: 372 pages

Best practices for designing, coding, and distributing your Python software

1. Learn Python development best practices from an expert, with detailed coverage of naming and coding conventions

2. Apply object-oriented principles, design patterns, and advanced syntax tricks

3. Manage your code with distributed version control

4. Profile and optimize your code

5. Proactive test-driven development and continuous integration

Professional Plone Development

ISBN: 978-1-847191-98-4   Paperback: 420 pages

Building robust, content-centric web applications with Plone 3, an open source Content Management System

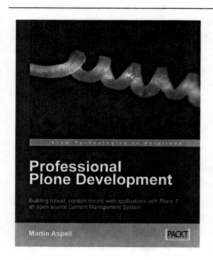

1. Plone development fundamentals

2. Customizing Plone

3. Developing new functionality

4. Real-world deployments

Please check **www.PacktPub.com** for information on our titles

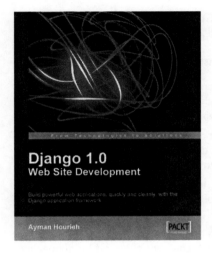

Django 1.0 Website Development

ISBN: 978-1-847196-78-1   Paperback: 272 pages

Build powerful web applications, quickly and cleanly, with the Django application framework

1. Teaches everything you need to create a complete Web 2.0-style web application with Django 1.0

2. Learn rapid development and clean, pragmatic design

3. No knowledge of Django required

4. Packed with examples and screenshots for better understanding

Grok 1.0 Web Development

ISBN: 978-1-847197-48-1   Paperback: 250 pages

Create flexible, agile web applications using the power of Grok—a Python web framework

1. Develop efficient and powerful web applications and web sites from start to finish using Grok, which is based on Zope 3

2. Integrate your applications or web sites with relational databases easily

3. Extend your applications using the power of the Zope Toolkit

4. Easy-to-follow and packed with practical, working code with clear explanations

Please check **www.PacktPub.com** for information on our titles

Django 1.1 Testing and Debugging

ISBN: 978-1-847197-56-6 Paperback: 430 pages

Building rigorously tested and bug-free Django applications

1. Develop Django applications quickly with fewer bugs through effective use of automated testing and debugging tools.

2. Ensure your code is accurate and stable throughout development and production by using Django's test framework.

3. Understand the working of code and its generated output with the help of debugging tools.

4. Packed with detailed working examples that illustrate the techniques and tools for debugging

Practical Plone 3

ISBN: 978-1-847191-78-6 Paperback: 592 pages

1. Get a Plone-based website up and running quickly without dealing with code

2. Beginner's guide with easy-to-follow instructions and screenshots

3. Learn how to make the best use of Plone's out-of-the-box features

4. Customize security, look-and-feel, and many other aspects of Plone

Please check **www.PacktPub.com** for information on our titles

Django 1.0 Template Development

ISBN: 978-1-847195-70-8   Paperback: 272 pages

A practical guide to Django template development with custom tags, filters, multiple templates, caching, and more

1. Dive into Django's template system and build your own template

2. Learn to use built-in tags and filters in Django 1.0

3. Practical tips for project setup and template structure

4. Use template techniques to improve your application's performance

Matplotlib for Python Developers

ISBN: 978-1-847197-90-0   Paperback: 308 pages

Build remarkable publication-quality plots the easy way

1. Create high quality 2D plots by using Matplotlib productively

2. Incremental introduction to Matplotlib, from the ground up to advanced levels

3. Embed Matplotlib in GTK+, Qt, and wxWidgets applications as well as web sites to utilize them in Python applications

4. Deploy Matplotlib in web applications and expose it on the Web using popular web frameworks such as Pylons and Django

5. Get to grips with hands-on code and complete realistic case study examples along with highly informative plot screenshots

Please check **www.PacktPub.com** for information on our titles

Lightning Source UK Ltd.
Milton Keynes UK
20 January 2010

148872UK00001B/82/P